ETHICAL ISSUES IN THE 21ST CENTURY

WHISTLEBLOWER PROTECTION AND RETALIATION ISSUES AT THE FBI

ETHICAL ISSUES IN THE 21ST CENTURY

Additional books in this series can be found on Nova's website
under the Series tab.

Additional e-books in this series can be found on Nova's website
under the e-book tab.

ETHICAL ISSUES IN THE 21ST CENTURY

WHISTLEBLOWER PROTECTION AND RETALIATION ISSUES AT THE FBI

EVELYN BROOKS
EDITOR

nova publishers
New York

Library of Congress Cataloging-in-Publication Data

ISBN: 978-1-63483-147-5

Published by Nova Science Publishers, Inc. † New York

CONTENTS

PREFACE

Whistleblowers help safeguard the federal government against waste, fraud, and abuse — however, they also risk retaliation by their employers. For example, in 2002, a former FBI agent allegedly suffered retaliation after disclosing that colleagues had stolen items from Ground Zero following the September 11, 2001, terrorist attacks. The Department of Justice (DOJ) found in her favor over 10 years after she reported the retaliation. The Government Accountability Office (GAO) reviewed DOJ's process for handling such complaints and in this book examines the time DOJ took to resolve FBI whistleblower retaliation complaints; the extent to which DOJ took steps to resolve complaints more quickly; and the extent to which DOJ complied with certain regulatory reporting requirements. Furthermore, in the context of the Intelligence Community (IC), whistleblowers are generally employees or contractors of federal intelligence agencies who bring to light information on agency wrongdoings. The threat of retaliation may deter potential whistleblowers from disclosing information on agency wrongdoing. There is seemingly tension between the desire to eliminate this deterrence, and thus encourage whistleblowers to bring agency misconduct to light, and the need to protect government secrets which, if disclosed publicly, could be harmful to the country's national security interests. This book concludes with a discussion on three sources of IC whistleblower protection against retaliation.

In: Whistleblower Protection …
Editor: Evelyn Brooks
ISBN: 978-1-63483-147-5

Chapter 1

WHISTLEBLOWER PROTECTION: ADDITIONAL ACTIONS NEEDED TO IMPROVE DOJ'S HANDLING OF FBI RETALIATION COMPLAINTS*

United States Government Accountability Office

WHY GAO DID THIS STUDY

Whistleblowers help safeguard the federal government against waste, fraud, and abuse—however, they also risk retaliation by their employers. For example, in 2002, a former FBI agent alleged she suffered retaliation after disclosing that colleagues had stolen items from Ground Zero following the September 11, 2001, terrorist attacks. DOJ found in her favor over 10 years after she reported the retaliation. GAO was asked to review DOJ's process for handling such complaints.

GAO examined (1) the time DOJ took to resolve FBI whistleblower retaliation complaints, (2) the extent to which DOJ took steps to resolve complaints more quickly, and (3) the extent to which DOJ complied with certain regulatory reporting requirements.

---

* This is an edited, reformatted and augmented version of the United States Government Accountability Office publication, GAO-15-112, dated January 2015.

GAO reviewed all DOJ case files for FBI whistleblower retaliation complaints DOJ closed from 2009 to 2013, and interviewed whistleblower attorneys, advocates, and government officials about the complaint process. The interview results are not generalizable.

What GAO Recommends

Congress may wish to consider whether FBI whistleblowers should have means to seek corrective action if retaliated against for disclosures to supervisors, among others. Further, GAO recommends that DOJ clarify guidance to clearly convey to whom employees can make protected disclosures, provide complainants with estimated complaint decision timeframes, and develop an oversight mechanism to monitor regulatory compliance. DOJ and the Office of the Inspector General concurred with GAO's recommendations.

What GAO Found

The Department of Justice (DOJ) closed 44 of the 62 (71 percent) Federal Bureau of Investigation (FBI) whistleblower retaliation complaints we reviewed within 1 year, took up to 4 years to close 15 complaints, and took up to 10.6 years to close the remaining 3. DOJ terminated 55 of the 62 complaints (89 percent) and awarded corrective action for 3. (Complainants withdrew 4.) We found that DOJ terminated many (48 of 62) complaints we reviewed because they did not meet certain regulatory requirements. For example, DOJ terminated at least 17 complaints in part because a disclosure was made to someone in the employee's chain of command or management, such as a supervisor, who was not one of the nine high-level FBI or DOJ entities designated under DOJ regulations to receive such disclosures. Unlike employees of other executive branch agencies, FBI employees do not have a process to seek corrective action if they experience retaliation based on a disclosure of wrongdoing to their supervisors or others in their chain of command who are not designated officials. This difference is due, in part, to DOJ's decisions about how to implement the statute governing FBI whistleblowers. In 2014, DOJ reviewed its regulations and, in an effort to balance competing priorities, recommended adding more senior officials in

FBI field offices to the list of designated entities, but did not recommend adding all supervisors. DOJ cited a number of reasons for this, including concerns about the additional resources and time needed to handle a possible increase in complaints if DOJ added supervisors. However, DOJ is already taking other steps to improve the efficiency of the complaint process. More importantly, dismissing retaliation complaints made to an employee's supervisor or someone in that person's chain of command leaves some FBI whistleblowers—such as the 17 complainants we identified—without protection from retaliation. By dismissing potentially legitimate complaints in this way, DOJ could deny some whistleblowers access to recourse, permit retaliatory activity to go uninvestigated, and create a chilling effect for future whistleblowers.

We also found that DOJ and FBI guidance is not always clear that FBI employees reporting alleged wrongdoing to a supervisor or someone in their chain of command may not be a protected disclosure. Ensuring that guidance always clearly explains to whom an FBI employee can report wrongdoing will help FBI whistleblowers ensure that they are fully protected from retaliation.

DOJ took from 2 to 10.6 years to resolve the 4 complaints we reviewed that DOJ adjudicated, and DOJ did not provide complainants with estimates of when to expect DOJ decisions throughout the complaint process. Providing such estimates would enhance accountability to complainants and provide additional assurance about DOJ management's commitment to improve efficiency.

Further, DOJ offices responsible for investigating whistleblower retaliation complaints have not consistently complied with certain regulatory requirements, such as obtaining complainants' approvals for extensions of time. One investigating office does not track investigators' compliance with specific regulatory requirements and does not have a formal oversight mechanism to do so. Effectively monitoring investigators' compliance with such requirements could help assure complainants that their cases are making progress and that they have the information they need to determine next steps for their complaints.

ABBREVIATIONS

DAG	Deputy Attorney General
DOD-OIG	Department of Defense Office of the Inspector General
DOJ	Department of Justice

DOJ-OPR	DOJ Office of Professional Responsibility
EEO	Equal Employment Opportunity
FBI	Federal Bureau of Investigation
FBI-INSD	FBI Inspection Division
MSPB	U.S. Merit Systems Protection Board
OARM	Office of Attorney Recruitment and Management
ODAG	Office of the Deputy Attorney General
OIG	Office of the Inspector General
OSC	U.S. Office of Special Counsel

* * *

January 23, 2015

The Honorable Charles E. Grassley
Chairman
Committee on the Judiciary
United States Senate

Dear Mr. Chairman:

Whistleblowers play an important role in safeguarding the federal government against waste, fraud, and abuse, and their willingness to come forward can contribute to improvements in government operations. However, whistleblowers also risk retaliation from their employers, sometimes being demoted, reassigned, or fired as a result of their actions. In 1998, the Department of Justice (DOJ) issued regulations that set forth the process for Federal Bureau of Investigation (FBI) whistleblowers to report complaints of retaliation for their disclosures.[1] These regulations require that FBI whistleblower retaliation complaints be directed to DOJ's Office of the Inspector General (OIG) or Office of Professional Responsibility (DOJ-OPR) for investigation and provide specific timeliness and reporting requirements for these offices to meet as they manage these complaints. The regulations also establish roles for the Director of DOJ's Office of Attorney Recruitment and Management (OARM) and the Deputy Attorney General (DAG). In some instances, the total process for resolving a complaint—including investigation, adjudication, and appeals—has taken several years. For example, in 2002, former FBI agent Jane Turner filed a whistleblower complaint with DOJ alleging that her colleagues had stolen items from Ground Zero after the

September 11, 2001, terrorist attacks. After making this whistleblower disclosure, she was given a "does not meet expectations" rating, placed on leave, and given a notice of proposed removal. According to Ms. Turner's attorneys, she retired from the FBI in order to avoid formal termination being placed on her record. Ms. Turner filed a whistleblower retaliation complaint that DOJ ultimately found in her favor in 2013—over 10 years later. Members of Congress and whistleblower advocates have raised questions about the length of time it takes DOJ to investigate and adjudicate FBI whistleblower retaliation complaints.

To assist Congress in overseeing DOJ's efforts to protect FBI whistleblowers, you asked us to examine DOJ's process for handling FBI whistleblower retaliation complaints. Specifically, our report examines:

- how long DOJ has taken to resolve FBI whistleblower retaliation complaints and what factors have affected these time frames;
- the extent to which DOJ has taken steps to resolve complaints more quickly and determine the impact of any such efforts; and
- the extent to which DOJ's OIG and DOJ-OPR have complied with regulatory reporting requirements.

To determine how long DOJ has taken to resolve FBI whistleblower retaliation complaints and the factors that affected these time frames, we reviewed DOJ case files for all FBI whistleblower retaliation complaints closed within the last 5 calendar years (from 2009 through 2013), and calculated the duration of each complaint from initial filing to appeal, as applicable; the length of time between interim steps throughout this process; and factors affecting the time frames in each case, among other things. Specifically, we reviewed a total of 62 closed cases representing 62 complaints. In addition, we reviewed documentation, such as internal procedures and memos, and interviewed senior DOJ officials in each of the four offices responsible for investigating or adjudicating whistleblower retaliation complaints—OIG, DOJ-OPR, OARM, and the Office of the Deputy Attorney General (ODAG)—about the factors that affected these time frames and DOJ's process for handling these complaints and compared aspects of this process against standards in *Standards for Internal Control in the Federal Government.*[2] Because of the sensitivity of FBI whistleblowers' identities, to obtain whistleblower perspectives on these issues, we met with representatives of five whistleblower advocacy groups knowledgeable about DOJ's process and attorneys who have represented three FBI whistleblowers through this process.[3] We identified the representatives of five whistleblower advocacy groups using an iterative process often referred to as snowball sampling. At each interview, we solicited names of additional groups to interview and selected for interviews those that were most widely recognized as knowledgeable about DOJ's process. The information we gathered from these groups and attorneys—referred to throughout our report collectively as eight whistleblower advocates and attorneys—is not generalizable, but provides perspectives on whistleblowers' experiences with DOJ's process.[4]

To determine the extent to which DOJ has taken steps to resolve complaints more quickly, we interviewed DOJ officials responsible for handling these complaints about the factors that affect the timely processing of these complaints and steps DOJ has taken to address them. In addition, to identify any practices that have improved timeliness in comparable federal settings, we interviewed senior officials in the Department of Defense Office of the Inspector General (DOD-OIG) as well as the U.S. Office of Special Counsel (OSC) and the U.S. Merit Systems Protection Board (MSPB)—federal agencies that handle whistleblower retaliation complaints for other federal employees—about those agencies' processes for handling whistleblower retaliation complaints. To identify the extent to which DOJ officials have taken steps to determine the impact of their efforts to improve timeliness, we interviewed DOJ officials and reviewed DOJ's April 2014 report to the President and compared DOJ's stated plans to standards in *Standards for Internal Control in the Federal Government*.[5]

To determine the extent to which OIG and DOJ-OPR have complied with regulatory reporting requirements, we compared evidence we saw in DOJ's case files with DOJ's regulations and analyzed the extent of any discrepancies. Specifically, for each case file, we reviewed the office's documented communication with the complainant including initial and ongoing outreach, and any interim and final notices that the agency closed or declined the case, as applicable. We also reviewed documentation and interviewed OIG and DOJ-OPR officials responsible for handling these complaints about any oversight mechanisms to ensure compliance with regulatory requirements. Further, we interviewed eight whistleblower advocates and attorneys, as noted above, to obtain whistleblower perspectives on the extent and effects of DOJ's compliance with regulatory requirements. In addition, because OSC serves a comparable function to that of OIG and DOJ-OPR in handling whistleblower complaints for most other federal employees and has similar regulatory reporting requirements, we interviewed OSC officials about their processes and mechanisms for ensuring compliance with OSC's requirements.

Additional details on our scope and methodology are discussed in appendix I.[6]

We conducted this performance audit from September 2013 through January 2015 in accordance with generally accepted government auditing standards. Those standards require that we plan and perform the audit to obtain sufficient, appropriate evidence to provide a reasonable basis for our findings and conclusions based on our audit objectives. We believe that the evidence obtained provides a reasonable basis for our findings and conclusions based on our audit objectives.

BACKGROUND

As established by the Civil Service Reform Act of 1978, federal law generally prohibits retaliation against federal government employees or applicants for employment for reporting wrongdoing, or whistleblowing.[7] Under these provisions, most federal employees pursue whistleblower retaliation complaints with OSC and MSPB. However, the FBI, as well as other intelligence agencies, is excluded from this process.[8] Instead, the Attorney General is required to establish regulations to ensure that FBI employees are protected against retaliation for reporting wrongdoing, consistent with certain statutory processes of OSC and MSPB.[9] Since the Civil Service Reform Act of 1978 was enacted, numerous amendments have been made to the provisions governing most executive branch whistleblowers, but corresponding amendments have generally not been made to the statutory provision governing FBI employees.[10] Provisions providing recourse for employees of intelligence community elements who are retaliated against for making disclosures of protected information were established by Presidential Policy Directive 19 in 2012,[11] and in statute in 2014.[12]

In order to implement the statute governing FBI whistleblower protections, in 1998, DOJ issued regulations to protect FBI whistleblowers from retaliation for reporting alleged wrongdoing, and established the process for handling FBI whistleblower retaliation complaints.[13] Specifically, the regulations prohibit DOJ employees from taking or failing to take (or threatening to take or fail to take) a personnel action with respect to any FBI employee as a reprisal for a protected disclosure (i.e., retaliation).[14] The regulations also define what disclosures by FBI employees qualify as protected disclosures, entitling the employees to recourse should they experience retaliation. Specifically, the regulations state that disclosures are protected if the complainants

1. reasonably believe that they are reporting wrongdoing, defined as a violation of any law, rule, or regulation; mismanagement; a gross waste of funds; an abuse of authority; or a substantial and specific danger to public health or safety,[15] and
2. report the alleged wrongdoing to one of nine designated officials or offices (e.g., the Attorney General, the DAG, and OIG, among other entities).[16]

If the FBI employee does not meet either of these two criteria, then that person's disclosure is not protected and the person does not have a right to recourse if the individual should experience retaliation as a result. That is, for example, if the person reports wrongdoing to a nondesignated entity and then experiences retaliation, the person will not be eligible for corrective action for that retaliation. Further, once the employee reported to a nondesignated entity and experienced retaliation as a result, the employee cannot subsequently report the alleged wrongdoing to a designated entity and obtain corrective action for the retaliation that has already taken place.

Division of Responsibility for FBI Whistleblower Retaliation Complaints

The regulations lay out DOJ's process for handling FBI whistleblower retaliation complaints and describe various offices' responsibilities for investigating, adjudicating, and reviewing appeals related to these complaints. See figure 1.

- **Investigation:** OIG and DOJ-OPR are responsible for receiving and investigating FBI whistleblower retaliation complaints to determine whether there are reasonable grounds to believe that a retaliatory act has been or will be taken ("reasonable grounds" determination).[17] The office that investigates the complaint (referred to as the investigating office) first reviews the complaint to determine whether it meets threshold regulatory requirements. A complaint that did not meet threshold regulatory requirements means a complaint where DOJ's decision to terminate the complaint was not based on whether there was a reprisal taken because of a disclosure, but on whether the allegations met threshold requirements. For example, the investigating office may determine that the complaint does not meet threshold regulatory requirements because the complainant did not make his or her underlying disclosure to one of the nine entities designated in the regulations; or because the alleged retaliatory personnel action occurred before the complainant made a protected disclosure and therefore could not have been caused by the protected disclosure. If the complaint does not meet threshold regulatory requirements, then the investigating office closes the complaint.[18] However, if the investigating office determines that the complaint met threshold regulatory requirements, then the office investigates the merits of the complaint by, for example, conducting interviews and requesting and reviewing documentation, such as employee statements and records from the FBI.[19] At the conclusion of an investigation, if OIG or DOJ-OPR finds that there are reasonable grounds, it then forwards its investigative report with any recommended actions to OARM for adjudication. In cases in which OIG or DOJ-OPR has not found in the complainant's favor or has not completed its investigation, the complainant may go directly to OARM to request corrective action.[20]

- **Adjudication:** OARM is responsible for adjudicating FBI whistleblower retaliation cases. OARM receives these cases from OIG or DOJ-OPR where either office has determined there are reasonable grounds to believe that there has been or will be reprisal for a protected disclosure, or else directly from the complainant.[21] As with the investigating offices, when OARM receives the complaint, OARM first determines whether the complaint meets threshold regulatory requirements, before proceeding to review the merits of the complaint. For OARM, considering the merits of the complaint entails reviewing the supporting evidence (e.g., documents and testimony), as well as the arguments each party—the complainant and the FBI—submits, and then determining, based on all of the evidence, if the individual substantiated the claim of retaliation. If the complaint is substantiated and the FBI is unable to prove by clear and convincing evidence that it would have taken the same personnel action even if the complainant had not made the protected disclosure, OARM will order that the FBI take corrective action, such as providing the complainant back pay or reimbursement for attorney's fees.

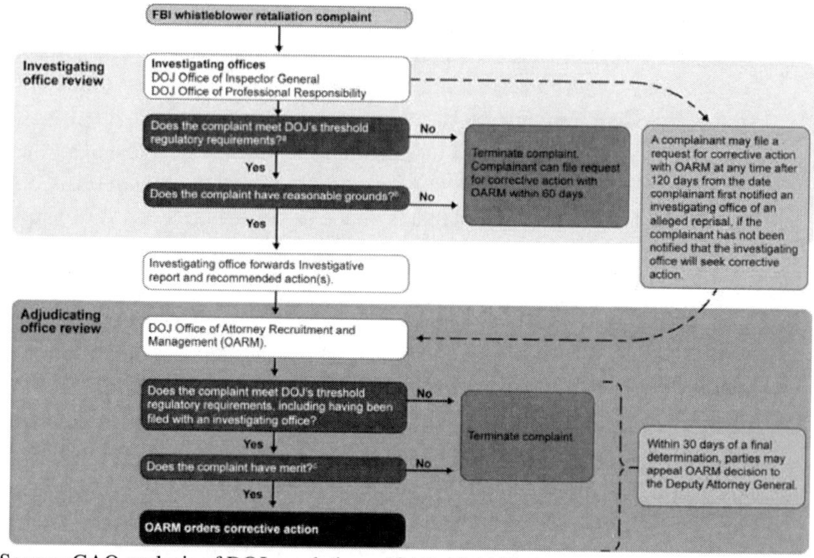

Source: GAO analysis of DOJ regulations. (GAO-15-112).

a A complaint that did not meet threshold regulatory requirements means a complaint where DOJ's decision to terminate the complaint was not based on whether there was a reprisal taken because of a disclosure, but on whether the allegations met threshold requirements. For example, threshold regulatory requirements include the requirement that the disclosure was made to one of nine designated entities, the alleged retaliatory act was a personnel action as defined by the regulations, and others.

b DOJ's Office of the Inspector General and Office of Professional Responsibility are required by DOJ regulation to determine whether there are reasonable grounds to believe that a reprisal has been or will be taken against the complainant.

c OARM determines whether, on the basis of a preponderance of the evidence, the employee made a protected disclosure, and if so, whether the disclosure was a contributing factor in the personnel action at issue. If the complainant meets that burden, then OARM considers whether the FBI has demonstrated by clear and convincing evidence that it would have taken the same personnel action in the absence of such disclosure.

Figure 1. The Department of Justice's (DOJ) Process for Investigating and Adjudicating Federal Bureau of Investigation (FBI) Whistleblower Retaliation Complaints.

- **Appeals:** DOJ's DAG is responsible for reviewing and ruling on parties' appeals of OARM decisions. Once OARM rules on a case, the parties have 30 days to file an appeal with the DAG. The DAG has the authority to set aside or modify OARM's decisions when found to be arbitrary, capricious, an abuse of discretion, or otherwise not in accordance with law; obtained without procedures required by law, rule, or regulation having been followed; or unsupported by substantial evidence. The DAG has full discretion to review and modify the corrective action ordered.[22]

DOJ's Regulatory Timeliness and Reporting Requirements

DOJ's regulations also set forth timeliness and reporting requirements for the investigating offices.[23] Specifically, the investigating offices must

- provide written notice to the complainant acknowledging receipt of the complaint within 15 calendar days of either investigating office receiving it;[24]
- update the complainant on the status of the investigation within 90 days of the written acknowledgment, and continue providing such updates every 60 days thereafter;[25] and
- determine within 240 calendar days of receiving the complaint whether there are reasonable grounds to believe that there has been or will be a reprisal for a protected disclosure, unless the complainant agrees to an extension.[26]

Additionally, if OIG or DOJ-OPR decides to terminate an investigation, the office must provide a written status report to the complainant at least 10 business days prior to the office's final termination report.[27] The final report must summarize the relevant facts of the case, provide reasons for terminating the investigation, and respond to any comments the complainant submits in response to the above-mentioned status report.[28]

DOJ Closed Majority of Complaints within a Year, Some Because Employee Did Not Report Wrongdoing to Designated Official; Complaints DOJ Adjudicated Took up to 10 Years

DOJ closed the majority of the 62 complaints we reviewed within 1 year, generally because the complaints did not meet DOJ's threshold regulatory requirements. The most common reason these complaints did not meet DOJ's threshold regulatory requirements was because the complainants made their disclosures to individuals or offices not designated in the regulations. Further, FBI whistleblowers may not be aware that they must report an allegation of wrongdoing to certain designated officials to qualify as a protected disclosure, in part because information DOJ has provided to its employees has not consistently explained to whom an employee must report protected disclosures. The 4 complaints we reviewed that met DOJ's threshold regulatory requirements and OARM ultimately adjudicated on the merits lasted from 2 to just over 10.6 years from the initial filing of the complaints with OIG or DOJ-OPR to the final OARM or DAG ruling. In some cases, parties have waited a year or more for a DOJ decision without information on when they might receive it. Figure 2 shows the duration and outcome of all 62 complaints we reviewed.

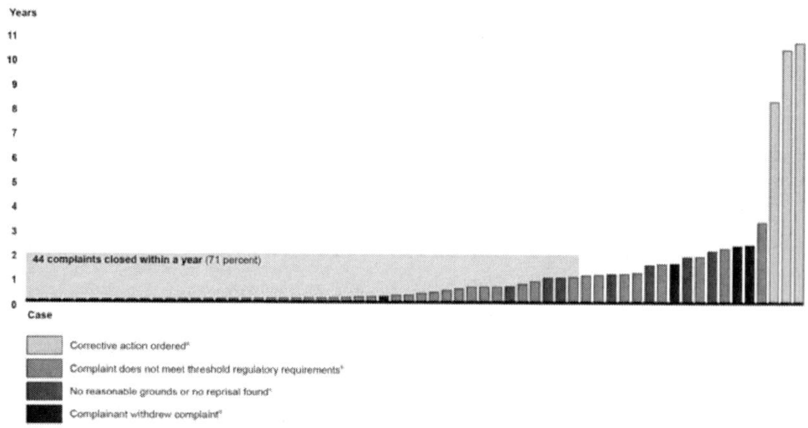

Source: GAO analysis of DOJ cases files. (GAO-15-112).

[a] In the 3 complaints we reviewed where DOJ's Office of Attorney Recruitment and Management (OARM) ordered corrective action, it did not always order all of the corrective action the complainant sought where OARM determined that the complainant failed to establish entitlement to the corrective relief sought under 28 C.F.R. § 27.4(f).

[b] The "does not meet threshold regulatory requirements" category includes 48 complaints ultimately found by either an investigating office or OARM as not meeting DOJ's threshold regulatory requirements because, for example, the disclosure was not made to one of nine designated entities or the alleged retaliatory act was not a personnel action as defined by the regulations.

[c] The "no reasonable grounds or no reprisal found" category includes 6 complaints where the investigating office opened an investigation into at least one allegation made by the complainant but the investigating office did not find reasonable grounds to believe that a reprisal had been or will be taken against the complainant. It also includes 1 complaint where OARM found the disclosure was not a contributing factor in the personnel action based on a preponderance of the evidence or the FBI demonstrated by clear and convincing evidence that it would have taken the same personnel action in the absence of such disclosure.

[d] The "complainant withdrew complaint" category includes 4 complaints that were voluntarily withdrawn by the complainant.

Figure 2. Overall Length of Complaints the Department of Justice (DOJ) Closed from 2009 to 2013 and Reasons for Case Closure.

DOJ Closed Majority of Complaints within a Year; Some Because the Employee Did Not Report Wrongdoing to a Designated Official

DOJ closed 44 of the 62 complaints (71 percent) that we reviewed within 1 year, most often because the complaint did not meet DOJ's threshold regulatory requirements. Specifically, for 40 of these 44 cases (91 percent), DOJ found that the complaint did not meet threshold regulatory requirements.[29] In 15 of the 32 (47 percent) complaints closed within a year where documentation in the case files was sufficient for us to determine why DOJ determined threshold requirements were not met, the fact that the complainant made a disclosure to the wrong person— someone not designated in the regulations to receive whistleblower complaints—was at least a partial basis for DOJ deciding the complaint did not meet threshold regulatory requirements.[30] In at least 12 of these 15 instances, the complainant reported the alleged wrongdoing to someone in management or within the complainant's chain of command, such as the complainant's supervisor, who was not one of the nine designated entities.[31]

For all 54 complaints we reviewed where documentation in the case files was sufficient for us to determine a specific reason DOJ closed the complaint, regardless of how long DOJ took to close the complaint, 23 (43 percent) had at least one claim dismissed because the complainant made his or her disclosure to an official or entity not designated in the regulations.[32] Of these, in at least 17 cases, we were able to determine that a disclosure was made to someone in the employee's chain of command or management.[33]

See appendix II for a summary of DOJ's final determinations in all cases we reviewed.

FBI Employees are Not Protected for Reporting Wrongdoing to Their Supervisors or Others in Their Chain of Command Not Designated in DOJ Regulations

Unlike employees of other executive branch agencies—including intelligence agencies—FBI employees do not have a process to seek corrective action if they experience retaliation based on a disclosure of wrongdoing to their supervisors or others in their chain of command who are not designated officials.[34] In 1978, federal law excluded the FBI, as well as other intelligence agencies, from the prohibited personnel practices system in place for employees of other executive branch agencies in part because of the sensitive nature of these agencies' operations and the information they handle. Instead the law required the Attorney General to develop regulations to ensure that FBI employees are not retaliated against for disclosures of wrongdoing.[35]

When issuing its interim and final regulations in 1998 and 1999, respectively, DOJ considered which individuals and offices the Attorney General would designate to receive protected disclosures from FBI employees. DOJ officials who developed these regulations included eight designated entities but did not include supervisors at that time because the officials maintained that Congress intended DOJ to limit the universe of recipients of protected disclosures, in part because of the sensitive information to which FBI employees have access.[36] In issuing its final rule, DOJ responded to commenter suggestions to add additional entities to receive such disclosures—including FBI-INSD, supervisors, and coworkers. Among other things, DOJ stated its view that Congress contemplated that recipients for whistleblower disclosures would be a relatively restricted group and "to designate a large (and in the case of supervisors, arguably ill-defined) group of employees as recipients would be inconsistent with Congress's decision, given the sensitivity of information to which FBI employees have access." In addition, DOJ's rule explained that "designating the highest ranking official in each field office, but not all supervisors, as recipients of protected disclosures . . . provides a way to channel such disclosures to those in the field who are in a position to respond and to correct management and other problems while also providing an on-site contact in the field for making protected disclosures."

In October 2012, the President issued Presidential Policy Directive 19, which established whistleblower protections for employees serving in the intelligence community, including, among other things, explicitly providing protection to employees who are retaliated against for reporting wrongdoing "to a supervisor in the employee's direct chain of command up to and including the head of the employing agency." Presidential Policy Directive 19 excluded the FBI from the scope of these protections, and instead required DOJ to report to the President on the efficacy of its regulations pertaining to FBI whistleblower retaliation and describe any proposed revisions to these regulations to increase their effectiveness.[37]

In response to this requirement, ODAG officials led an effort to review FBI whistleblower retaliation complaints filed from January 1, 2005, through March 15, 2014, and, consistent with our review, found that DOJ had terminated a significant portion of complaints because they were not made to the proper individual or office. In addition, DOJ officials met with whistleblower advocates and OSC officials to solicit their views and found that these individuals and officials recommended that DOJ broaden its regulations to protect disclosures to any supervisor in the employee's chain of command. According to DOJ's April 2014 report in response to Presidential Policy Directive 19, the whistleblower advocates noted that the directive instructs intelligence community elements to protect disclosures to any supervisor in the employee's direct chain of command and that this is consistent with whistleblower protection laws that similarly protect other civil service employees. Further, DOJ's report notes that OSC officials believe that to deny employees protection unless their disclosure is made to the high-ranked supervisors in the office would undermine a central purpose of whistleblower protection laws.

In response to PPD-19, DOJ officials led by ODAG revisited their 1999 regulations and in April 2014 recommended expanding the persons to whom individuals can make protected disclosures to include—in addition to the highest-ranking official in FBI field offices, who is already included—the second highest ranking tier of officials in these field offices, which includes the two or three assistant special agents in charge in 53 field offices and the special agents in charge in the 3 largest field offices. Senior DOJ officials told us that DOJ leadership has approved this change and the agency is beginning the public notice and comment process; as of December 2014, DOJ has not issued any notice of proposed rulemaking or publicly moved forward on these stated plans. DOJ officials reported that they plan to evaluate the impact of this expansion, and they may choose subsequently to further expand the set of persons to whom an employee can make a protected disclosure, if DOJ determines that such expansion is warranted. However, as of December 2014, senior FBI and ODAG officials report that they do not have an estimated date or specific plans for this evaluation and could not provide specifics on how this evaluation would be conducted.

DOJ officials gave us several explanations about why DOJ did not recommend expanding the list to include supervisors and others in the employee's chain of command, a change that would bring the FBI into line with other executive branch agencies. First, in DOJ's April 2014 report, DOJ officials state that "the Department believes the set of persons to whom a protected disclosure can be made is extensive and diverse, and has seen no indication that the list has impeded disclosures of wrongdoing." However, when we asked officials how they arrived as this conclusion—particularly in light of our and DOJ's previous findings that numerous complainants had at least one claim dismissed for making a disclosure to someone in management or their chain of command— they could not provide supporting evidence or analysis for their conclusions. Rather, these officials cited concerns about striking the right balance between the benefits of an expanded list and the level of resources the department would have to expend assessing more complaints if the department added more designated officials, and the potential impact of these additional complaints on the timeliness of the process. While DOJ's focus on the timeliness of complaint processing is important, dismissing retaliation complaints made to an employee's supervisor or someone in his or her chain of command who is not a designated entity leaves some FBI whistleblowers with no recourse if they experience retaliation. We found at least 17 whistleblowers whose cases were dismissed—at least in part—for making a disclosure of wrongdoing to someone in their chain of command or management.[38] Our findings are similar to those of the ODAG-led review in which the department found that in a "significant portion" of OIG cases the claim was closed because it was not made to a proper individual or office under the regulations.[39] This means that these employees had no recourse for retaliation they may have experienced for making those disclosures. Moreover, with respect to DOJ's concerns about resources and timeliness, DOJ has discretion in determining its regulatory process for enforcing protections for FBI whistleblowers and, as described in more detail later this report, is taking other steps to improve the timeliness of the process.

Senior FBI and ODAG officials also explained that the department plans to provide FBI employees with additional training on the list of entities designated to receive whistleblower complaints. While training could help provide information on how to make a protected disclosure, this planned training would have little effect for employees who initially raise a concern to their supervisors not expecting that this action would ever be a whistleblower disclosure. All seven of the whistleblower advocates and attorneys we interviewed who had relevant personal and professional experience stated that it is common practice for employees to report wrongdoing to their supervisors before reporting it to a more senior official, such as those designated in DOJ's regulations.[40] Further, two advocates we met with stressed that very few people intend to become whistleblowers. Rather, it is typical for employees who become aware of a problem to report it to their supervisors, expecting to resolve the issue at that level. In one FBI whistleblower case file we reviewed, the complainant wrote that "there is a practice in the FBI that a person is to go through his or her chain of command first." Further, senior FBI officials we spoke with emphasized that FBI policy encourages employees to report allegations of wrongdoing to a broader group of entities than those designated in regulation as recipients of protected disclosures—including any supervisor in the chain of command of the person reporting.[41]

Last, senior FBI and ODAG officials noted that the statute establishing whistleblower protections for FBI employees differs from the statute governing protections for other federal employees, so there is no legal requirement that DOJ designate supervisors or others in an employee's chain of command to receive protected disclosures. The separate statutory provision for the FBI has existed since enactment of the CSRA in 1978, but has generally not been revisited by Congress when passing amendments to legislation governing other executive branch whistleblowers. Over the years, Congress has passed amendments to the legislation covering employees in other executive branch agencies that explicitly strengthen and expand protections for other federal whistleblowers. For example, Congress added language clarifying that disclosures to supervisors who participated in the misconduct are protected disclosures. The Whistleblower Act of 1989 provides, among other things, that employees should not suffer adverse consequences as a result of prohibited personnel practices.[42] The Senate report accompanying the Whistleblower Protection Enhancement Act of 2012 explained that, with regard to whistleblower retaliation matters, the focus should not be on whether or not disclosures of wrongdoing were protected, but rather whether the personnel action at issue in the case occurred because of the protected disclosure.[43] However, changes to laws affecting other executive branch whistleblowers did not automatically extend to the FBI since the law governing FBI employees was in a separate provision of the original legislation. DOJ's current regulations and its recommended changes deny FBI employees protection provided to employees of other executive branch agencies—including those in the intelligence community.[44] Thus, DOJ risks dismissing, and potentially not addressing, instances of actual retaliation against individuals who reported their disclosure to their supervisors, or another entity not designated in the regulations. Dismissing these whistleblower retaliation complaints could deny whistleblowers access to recourse, could permit retaliatory activity to go uninvestigated, and may have a chilling effect on other potential whistleblowers.

DOJ Guidance Is Not Always Clear

In the course of our review, in addition to several DOJ and FBI guidance documents that accurately describe DOJ's FBI whistleblower regulations, we also found instances of DOJ guidance that could lead FBI employees to believe that reporting an allegation of wrongdoing to a supervisor in their chain of command would be a protected disclosure when that is not the case.[45] First, FBI's guidance—the *FBI Domestic Investigations and Operations Guide*, specifically—states that, in general, the FBI requires employees to report known or suspected failures to adhere to the law, rules, or regulations to any supervisor in the employees' chain of command, or others, but does not clarify that such disclosures are protected only if reported to certain designated individuals or offices.[46] Second, an April 2014 memo from the DAG to all DOJ employees— including FBI employees—encouraged employees to watch a video on whistleblower rights and protections and stated that employees may report waste, fraud, or abuse within the department to supervisors within their offices or the OIG, or outside the department to OSC.[47] The memo did not clarify that FBI employees who report such allegations to their supervisors or OSC may not have the right to pursue corrective action should they experience retaliation for their disclosure. Senior ODAG officials acknowledged that if taken in isolation, this memo could cause some confusion for FBI employees but stressed that FBI employees should already be familiar with the FBI-specific policy from FBI-offered training and resources. However, we reviewed the two trainings FBI officials cited as educating FBI employees on the procedures to follow when making a whistleblower complaint, and neither training mentions DOJ's regulations related to FBI whistleblower retaliation or the specific steps FBI employees need to take to ensure their disclosures are protected.[48] OIG and FBI officials report that they are currently developing a training video that will address FBI-specific issues and will be required for all FBI employees. This planned training could improve employee awareness of the FBI-specific procedures, but such an effort could be undercut if unclear written policies and communications continue to be provided to FBI employees.

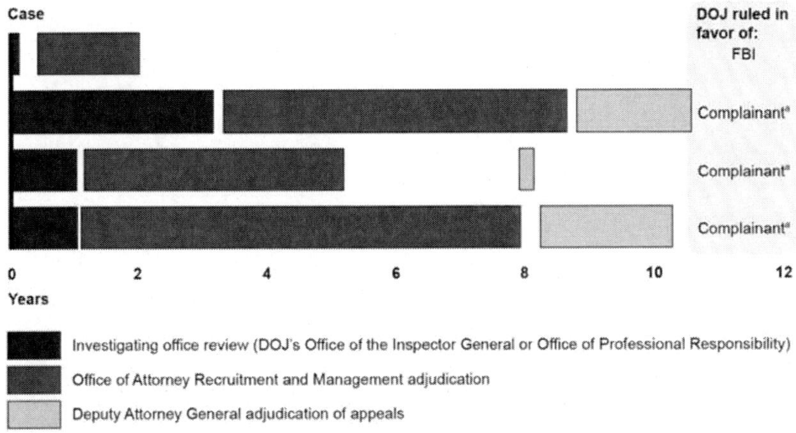

Source: GAO analysis of DOJ case files. GAO-15-112

Notes: For the investigating office's review, the graph reflects the time between the date the investigating office received the complaint and the date the office sent a termination report to the complainant (or in 1 case the date the complainant informed the investigating office that the complainant intended to go to OARM after receiving the proposed termination report). For OARM's adjudication, the graph reflects the time between the date the complainant filed a request for corrective action with OARM and OARM's final decision or corrective action order, whichever was later. For the Deputy Attorney General's adjudication of appeals, the graph reflects the time between the first party's appeal following OARM's final decision and the final adjudication on any appeals associated with that case. Each phase depicted in the graph includes all activity during that phase, such as extensions of time requested by the parties and time awaiting DOJ decisions. The gaps in the bars reflect time between the conclusion of one office's handling of the case and the complainant—or FBI in the case of some appeals—bringing the complaint to the attention of the next office.

[a] In these cases, DOJ ruled in favor of the complainant on at least one claim, but not necessarily on all of the complainant's claims.

Figure 3. Length of Cases the Department of Justice (DOJ) Adjudicated, in Years.

Standards for Internal Control in the Federal Government provides that agencies should distribute pertinent information so employees may efficiently carry out their duties.[49] Without clear information on the process for making a protected disclosure, including the individuals to whom a claimant can make a protected disclosure, FBI whistleblowers may not be aware that, depending on how they report their allegation, they may not be able to seek corrective action should they experience retaliation.

DOJ Took up to 10 Years to Resolve the 4 Complaints It Adjudicated on the Merits and Did Not Provide Parties with Expected Time Frames for Its Decisions

OARM adjudicated the merits of 4 of the 62 complaints we reviewed (6 percent), and these 4 cases lasted from 2 to just over 10.6 years, from the initial filing of the complaints with OIG or DOJ-OPR to the final OARM or ODAG ruling.[50] In 3 of these 4 cases, DOJ ultimately ruled in favor of the whistleblower. As shown in figure 3, these 3 cases lasted from just over 8 to 10.6 years. In the fourth case, DOJ ruled in favor of the FBI and this case lasted approximately 2 years.

According to DOJ officials responsible for handling these complaints, case-specific factors, including competing staff priorities at any given time, case complexity, and parties' requests for extensions, affected the length of investigating and adjudicating complaints.

- **Competing priorities:** These OIG, DOJ-OPR, OARM, and ODAG officials report that competing priorities for staff and senior management attention affect the length of FBI whistleblower retaliation cases. For example, a senior ODAG official explained that competing priorities is the biggest factor affecting the timeliness of ODAG's handling of appeals. This official explained that the DAG (who, under DOJ's regulations, personally decides on appeals) and ODAG staff (who prepare the DAG to discuss and decide the matter) handle issues of national importance and security so the office often has more time-sensitive and important issues that delay its decisions on FBI whistleblower retaliation cases. [51] The ODAG officials explained that to address this in part, in September 2014, they finalized an agreement to obtain assistance from Justice Management Division attorneys on future FBI whistleblower retaliation appeals, but ODAG officials acknowledged that this will not address the issue of competing priorities for the DAG. Further, we reviewed some OIG and DOJ-OPR investigative case files that included no evidence of agency activity for as long as 8 months for OIG and 12 months for DOJ-OPR. OIG and DOJ-OPR officials cited competing priorities—for the Inspector General and for the assigned investigator, respectively—as the biggest factor affecting the identified periods of apparent inactivity. Senior ODAG and OIG officials stress that the fact that the DAG and Inspector General personally review each complaint highlights the importance these offices place on these complaints, but note that competing priorities for these individuals' time do result in delays.

- **Case complexity:** OIG, DOJ-OPR, and OARM officials report that case complexity—such as numerous disclosures and allegations of retaliation, many witnesses, and voluminous documents—can cause a case to take longer. At the investigation stage, case complexity increases the need for cooperation and information from various people involved, including the complainant, witnesses, and the FBI—all of which can contribute to the length of the investigation, according to DOJ-OPR officials. OARM officials report that, at the adjudication stage, case complexity is a major factor affecting how quickly they can consider all of the relevant evidence and write decisions.
- **Parties' requests for extensions:** Once a case is at the adjudication stage, the FBI or the complainant may request extensions of time, such as an extension of an OARM deadline to collect evidence. In 9 of 16 cases we reviewed that OARM or ODAG handled, parties filed a total of 69 requests for extensions—the FBI requested 43, complainants requested 19, and 7 were joint requests.[52] The median length of extensions that both the FBI and complainants requested was 15 days. In the 4 adjudicated cases shown in figure 3, parties' requests for extensions accounted for 45 days of the shortest case and over 19 months of the longest case.

In addition to affecting overall case length, competing priorities and case complexity specifically affect how long OARM and ODAG take to issue individual decisions on whether complaints met threshold regulatory requirements, merits, and appeals throughout the process. In the cases we reviewed, the longest wait for a decision was just over a year and a half for OARM to issue a decision on the merits of a case and the shortest was 4 days for OARM to rule on whether a complaint met threshold regulatory requirements.[53] Parties at some point waited a year or more for a decision by either OARM or ODAG in 6 of 15 complaints we reviewed that progressed to the point of an OARM decision on whether the complaint met threshold regulatory requirements.

OARM and ODAG do not routinely provide parties with an estimate for when they expect to return decisions in these cases, though OARM officials responsible for handling these complaints report that they have provided estimates in some cases where the parties specifically requested them. These OARM officials explained that they do not routinely provide such estimates because time frames can be difficult to judge, in part because of the complexity of the cases and the volume of evidence. Similarly, senior ODAG officials stated that such estimates would be guesses that could raise expectations the offices cannot meet because, for example, they cannot predict the Deputy Attorney General's schedule.

Other federal agencies and offices that handle whistleblower retaliation cases provide complainants with an estimate for when their cases will conclude. MSPB—which DOJ officials have looked to in the past for best practices in handling whistleblower retaliation cases—is statutorily required to provide parties with an estimate for when MSPB will make a decision. Accordingly, MSPB developed a goal to decide cases in 120 days, and where MSPB officials anticipate missing this goal by 30 days or more, it is MSPB's policy to publicly announce a new date for completion.[54] Legislative history suggests that this requirement was intended to reduce delays.[55] Similarly, DOD-OIG is statutorily required to complete reports of its investigations into whistleblower retaliation complaints within 180 days, and if officials need additional time, they must inform the complainant as to why and provide a new date by which the investigation report will be completed.[56] A senior DOD-OIG official told us that, at a minimum, a status update regarding progress toward case completion provides the complainant with an element of assurance that the case is being actively worked on and has not slipped through the cracks. An estimate also reinforces a sense of urgency and serves as an accountability measure for DOD-OIG investigative personnel, who understand that individuals with great interest in the outcome of the investigation are expecting timely results, according to the DOD official.

Further, all eight whistleblower advocates and attorneys we met with agreed that it would be helpful for DOJ to provide such estimates. Six of the advocates and attorneys we met with explained that not having an estimate for when OARM or ODAG will return a decision in these cases may hurt complainants' morale and confidence in the process. Further, five advocates and attorneys noted that other FBI employees witness the uncertainty and professional limbo whistleblowers experience while DOJ considers a whistleblower retaliation complaint, and five further noted that this potentially has a chilling effect on prospective whistleblowers.

In February 2013 two of the advocacy groups we interviewed—the American Civil Liberties Union and the National Whistleblowers Center—sent a memo to the Attorney General asking DOJ to require that OARM issue merit decisions within 90 days and the DAG issue appeals decisions within 60 days, among other changes. In its April 2014 report to the President, DOJ officials responded to this recommendation, stating that the department does not support these revisions at this time because, given the volume of evidence and complexity of these cases, it would be very difficult, if not impossible, to meet a strict deadline for adjudication. We understand that given the great variability among these cases, a single fixed deadline may be impractical, but this limitation should not preclude these offices from providing complainants with case- specific estimates that take into account the specifics of each particular complaint.

In June 2012, DOJ stated a commitment to making every effort to improve the efficiency of the department's adjudication of these complaints.[57] Internal control standards reinforce the position that agencies need to have ways of ensuring such management directives are carried out.[58] Providing parties with estimated time frames for returning DOJ's decisions in FBI whistleblower retaliation cases (whether a complaint meets threshold regulatory requirements, merits, and appeals) and timely updates when OARM and ODAG officials cannot meet estimated time frames would enhance accountability to the complainants and provide additional assurance about DOJ management's commitment to improve efficiency.

DOJ Officials Have Taken Some Steps to Resolve Complaints More Quickly but Have Limited Plans to Assess Impact

In the last 3 years, and in light of the Presidential Policy Directive 19 requirement that DOJ assess the efficacy of its current process, DOJ officials have identified some opportunities to improve their timeliness in resolving whistleblower retaliation complaints and have taken some steps to do so. However, DOJ officials have limited plans to assess the impacts of these actions. Specifically, OARM has developed a mediation program, hired an additional staff person, and developed procedures with stricter time frames, while DOJ-OPR and OIG have taken steps to streamline their intake procedures. DOJ leadership is also considering taking steps to revise DOJ's regulations to streamline OARM's process upon receiving a new complaint.

- **Developing a mediation program:** In the spring of 2014, OARM launched an alternative dispute resolution program that will provide complainants with the option to pursue mediation with the FBI at any point from initial filing of the complaint to appeal. OARM officials anticipate that this option will help to expedite processing of some complaints that can be more quickly resolved through mediation and permit DOJ to focus limited resources on the remaining cases. As of October 1, 2014, two complainants had pursued mediation, but, according to OARM officials, because these cases are pending, it is too soon to analyze the impact of the mediation program.[59]
- **Hiring additional staff:** To reduce the impact of competing priorities for limited staff, in November 2013, OARM senior officials stated that they hired a part-time attorney to help write OARM decisions in FBI whistleblower retaliation cases. OARM officials report that they have been able to reduce overall case-processing times, in good part because of the work of the part-time attorney.[60]
- **Developing procedures with stricter time frames:** Senior OARM officials report that in June 2011 they met with an MSPB administrative judge and an MSPB senior executive to gather ideas for shortening the time frames in OARM's cases. These officials further report that in response to the input from MSPB, in October of that same year OARM issued procedures that included stricter time frames for the complainant and FBI, such as shortening the period of time OARM initially provides for parties to gather evidence. In addition, OARM officials report that around this same time, they revised their practice of generally approving parties' requests for extensions. The OARM officials report that they began reviewing requests for an extension more critically and often do not approve the full length of the extension requested.
- **Streamlining intake procedures:** Senior OIG officials report that they could improve their timeliness in processing initial complaints and have since taken steps to ensure that complaints are transmitted for initial review within 1 to 2 days of receipt, if possible. DOJ-OPR officials report that in the last 2 years, they have established a new

intake procedure so that an intake attorney handles the initial notice to the whistleblower instead of waiting until the complaint is assigned to an investigator.

- **Streamlining OARM's process:** DOJ's April 2014 report to the President included a recommendation intended to expedite OARM's process upon receiving new complaints. DOJ's report states: "Under OARM's current process, when a complainant files a request for corrective action with OARM, OARM usually forwards it to the FBI and provides the FBI 25 calendar days to file its response. In some instances, however, the allegations in a complainant's request are so deficient that neither OARM nor the FBI can reasonably construe the specific claims raised." Under the recommended revised procedures, where it appears that a complaint may not meet DOJ's threshold regulatory requirements, OARM would give the complainant a very short time period to clarify why the case should not be dismissed. DOJ officials state that this could allow for quick resolution of cases that plainly fail to meet the threshold regulatory requirements and increase efficiency of case adjudication.

As DOJ implements these changes intended to improve the efficiency of DOJ's handling of FBI whistleblower retaliation complaints, as detailed above, assessing the impact would help DOJ officials ensure that these changes are in fact shortening total case length without sacrificing quality, and identify any additional opportunities to improve efficiency. OARM officials report that given the length of these cases, it is too early to assess whether the efforts implemented thus far are having the desired impact on the timeliness of OARM's adjudication process, but they explained that in the future, they could use their case docket to determine impact. For example, they could review the number of cases resolved through mediation and whether the revised procedures from 2011 have made a difference in the time needed to adjudicate large cases. OARM's stated plans to monitor the impact is a good first step by one of the relevant offices, but assessing the impact on timeliness and quality throughout the entire investigation, adjudication, and appeal process to determine the impact on total complaint-processing time will require a joint effort among OIG, DOJ-OPR, OARM, and ODAG.

In DOJ's April 2014 report to the President, DOJ stated plans to evaluate the impact of two policy changes to increase the effectiveness of DOJ's regulations, but stated no such plans for the policy changes intended to improve DOJ's timeliness in handling these complaints. *Standards for Internal*

Control in the Federal Government calls for agencies to compare actual performance with planned or expected results and analyze significant differences.[61] Without assessing the impact of its policy changes on the complete process, DOJ will not be in a position to gauge progress in fulfilling DOJ's commitment to improving its efficiency in handling these complaints and correct course, if needed. Without assessment, it will be difficult for DOJ to know whether its various efforts to improve timeliness are working as intended.

OIG and DOJ-OPR Have Not Consistently Met Regulatory Requirements to Provide Complainants with Information Needed to Determine Next Steps for Their Complaints

OIG and DOJ-OPR Have Not Consistently Provided Complainants with Required Status Updates and Extension Requests; OIG Has Begun Tracking Compliance, but DOJ- OPR Has Not OIG and DOJ-OPR have not consistently provided complainants with status updates or obtained the complainant's approval for an extension when the investigator reviewing the complaint needed more time, as stipulated under agency regulations. In the last 2 years, OIG developed a database to increase management oversight of investigators' compliance with requirements to provide updates and obtain the complainants' approval for extensions, but DOJ-OPR does not have a similar mechanism in place. In addition, OIG did not inform complainants of its intent before closing complaints it declined to investigate and did not consistently explain the basis for its decisions to complainants, but plans to begin doing so.

OIG and DOJ-OPR Have Not Consistently Provided Complainants with Required Status Updates and Extension Requests; OIG Has Begun Tracking Compliance, but DOJ-OPR Has Not

OIG and DOJ-OPR have not consistently provided complainants with periodic status updates nor have they always obtained complainants' approvals for extensions when the investigator reviewing the complaint needed more time, as required under DOJ's FBI whistleblower regulations.[62] Specifically, in

65 percent of the complaints we reviewed (37 of 57), the investigating office did not meet the regulatory requirement to contact the complainant to acknowledge that the office had received the complaint within 15 days of the date either OIG or DOJ-OPR received the complaint. In particular, OIG did not meet the requirement in 20 of 36 complaints (56 percent) and DOJ-OPR did not meet the requirement in 17 of 21 complaints (81 percent). See appendix III for more detail on the number and percentage of complaints in which OIG and DOJ-OPR met each reporting requirement.

After the deadline to acknowledge that the office received the complaint, we saw evidence in the case files for the majority of complaints we reviewed (27 of 37, or 73 percent) that OIG and DOJ-OPR provided the first status update within the 90-day time frame; however, both offices were less consistent about meeting the time frames for subsequent status updates, which are required at least every 60 days.[63] In 20 of 27 complaints we reviewed (74 percent)—including 8 of 12 OIG complaints and 12 of 15 DOJ-OPR complaints—we saw at least one period of more than 60 days during which the case file did not contain evidence that the investigating office had communicated with the complainant. In 8 of these 20 complaints, we identified only one 60-day period in which the case file did not contain evidence of communication with the complainant. However, in the other 12 complaints, we identified more than one 60-day period in which the case file did not demonstrate that the investigating office had communicated with the complainant.

In addition, OIG and DOJ-OPR did not always obtain the complainant's approval for an extension when the investigator needed more time. As discussed previously, the regulations require that the investigating office determine within 240 days of receiving the complaint if there are reasonable grounds to believe whistleblower retaliation occurred, unless the complainant agrees to an extension.[64] We found that the investigating offices met this requirement in most of the complaints we reviewed (47 of 57, or 82 percent), generally because the offices closed the majority of complaints within 240 days (40 of 57, or 70 percent).[65] However, the case files for over half (10 of 17) of the complaints that exceeded 240 days— including 6 of 7 OIG complaints and 4 of 10 DOJ-OPR complaints—did not contain documentation that the complainant had agreed to an extension.

The regulatory requirements help ensure that both complainants and the investigating office receive information necessary to make decisions regarding the complaint. For example, the requirement to send notice to the complainant within 15 days acknowledging that the office has received the complaint ensures that the complainant is aware of whom to contact within OIG or DOJ-OPR if he or she has questions or additional information to provide regarding their complaint. Further, three of the eight whistleblower advocates and attorneys we spoke with stated that regular communication between investigators and complainants ensures that complainants provide the investigating office with follow-up information that the office needs to make a timely and appropriate decision. In addition, as previously discussed, the regulations provide complainants the right to bring their complaints directly to OARM after 120 days if they have not received notice that the investigating office will seek corrective action. Two of the whistleblower advocates we spoke with said that it is generally beneficial to the complainant to wait for OIG or DOJ-OPR to complete their investigations so that these offices can obtain a complete factual record, which is helpful if the complainant pursues his or her case with OARM. However, according to these whistleblower advocates, if the complainant is not satisfied with the investigating office's progress, the complainant may prefer to go directly to OARM. Regulatory requirements to provide periodic status updates and receive the complainant's approval for an extension when investigations are running long helps ensure complainants have the information they need to make this decision.

More broadly, regular status updates provide reassurance to complainants during the investigative process. Four of the eight whistleblower advocates and attorneys we spoke with said that regular status updates reassure complainants that the investigating office is continuing to make progress on their complaints. Further, six of the attorneys and advocates said that, without regular status updates, complainants can become discouraged and develop a negative view of the process. Five of these attorneys and advocates said that, as a result of these negative experiences, potential whistleblowers may be less likely to come forward to report wrongdoing.

At the time the case files we reviewed were open, OIG and DOJ-OPR did not have oversight mechanisms in place to ensure compliance with the status update and extension requirements. According to senior OIG officials and a DOJ-OPR official responsible for managing these complaints, managers regularly discussed individual complaints with the investigator assigned to the complaint, but the investigator was responsible for setting due dates to ensure compliance with the regulations. The OIG and DOJ-OPR officials we spoke with said that their investigators were frequently in communication with complainants, but these communications were not always documented within their case files. Without documentation of these communications, managers could not verify that investigators had communicated with complainants, as required. In addition, senior OIG officials and the DOJ-OPR official said that they maintained information on the dates whistleblower retaliation complaints were opened and closed within their case management systems; however, these systems were not specific to whistleblower retaliation complaints and did not contain dates of interim communications. As a result, managers could not use these systems to oversee investigators' compliance with requirements to provide status updates within prescribed time frames or obtain the complainant's approval for an extension, if required.

OIG has taken steps to begin tracking compliance with these requirements; however, DOJ-OPR has not yet taken similar action. Specifically, in July 2014, during the course of our review, an OIG manager informed staff responsible for these complaints of the importance of documenting status updates within case files to ensure documentation of OIG's compliance with regulatory requirements to update complainants within prescribed time frames. Further, over the last 2 years, OIG has developed a database it now uses as a management tool to oversee investigators' compliance with requirements for communicating with complainants. According to senior OIG officials we spoke with, OIG decided to develop this database to help ensure that OIG meets its regulatory requirements. OIG managers use the database to track dates of interim communications, such as status updates, and the database calculates regulatory deadlines for subsequent updates and for closing the complaint. In addition, according to senior OIG officials, managers can use the database to run reports, such as to see upcoming deadlines for all open complaints. Although it is too soon to tell how effective this database will be, if used consistently, this database could help OIG managers ensure investigators communicate with complainants in accordance with regulatory requirements.

According to a DOJ-OPR official responsible for managing these complaints, DOJ-OPR could place an even greater emphasis on the deadlines for these complaints and take additional steps to oversee communications with complainants. This official stated that DOJ-OPR investigators may lose track of deadlines for status updates in FBI whistleblower retaliation cases because similar requirements are not in place for other cases DOJ-OPR typically handles. Further, as discussed previously, in many of the case files we reviewed we did not see evidence of communication between the DOJ-OPR investigator and the complainant within required time frames. For example, in one case file we reviewed, the complainant listed numerous attempts to contact DOJ-OPR over the prior year and expressed frustration at not receiving the required status updates.

According to senior DOJ-OPR officials, DOJ-OPR has taken some steps to improve its management of whistleblower retaliation cases, but does not track investigators' compliance with specific regulatory requirements and does not have a formal oversight mechanism to do so. In the last year and a half, DOJ-OPR managers have started to receive weekly reports with information on all open complaints, according to a DOJ-OPR official responsible for managing these complaints. However, the official said that the reports do not contain information on status updates. A senior DOJ-OPR official reported that DOJ-OPR is in the initial stages of upgrading its case management system, and DOJ-OPR officials expect that the new system could eventually be tailored to allow them to capture additional information on the office's handling of FBI whistleblower retaliation complaints, such as the dates of communications between investigators and complainants.

Standards for Internal Control in the Federal Government calls for agencies to conduct ongoing monitoring in the course of normal operations, such as when investigating whistleblower retaliation complaints, to help managers ensure compliance with applicable regulations and achieve desired results.[66] DOJ-OPR has begun taking steps to upgrade its case management system but is very early in this process. As DOJ-OPR upgrades its case management system, tailoring the system to capture data specific to FBI whistleblower retaliation complaints, or developing some other mechanism, could provide DOJ- OPR managers and investigators information necessary to track compliance with regulatory requirements. Further, using that information to conduct ongoing monitoring of DOJ-OPR attorneys' compliance with regulatory requirements could help DOJ-OPR ensure complainants receive the periodic updates that they are entitled to and that they need to determine next steps for their complaints.

OIG Has Not Informed Complainants before Closing Complaints It Declined to Investigate or Consistently Communicated Reasons for Its Decision, but Plans to Begin Doing So

OIG has not informed complainants before closing complaints it declines to investigate and has not always communicated the reasons for its decision not to investigate because, according to senior OIG officials, OIG does not view the regulations as requiring them to do so. Specifically, these officials said that the regulations state that the office must provide the complainant with a written statement that indicates the office's intention to close the complaint when the investigating office decides to terminate an investigation. As a result, according to these officials, this provision does not apply if OIG declines the complaint before initiating an investigation. Similarly, these officials said that OIG does not view the requirement to send a final termination report including a summary of relevant facts and the reasons for terminating an investigation as applying to complaints OIG declines to investigate. Unlike in OIG's process, a DOJ-OPR official responsible for managing these complaints said that DOJ-OPR provides a draft report to the complainant when DOJ-OPR decides to close a complaint, including when DOJ-OPR makes this decision without initiating an investigation.

We found that OIG provided a proposed termination report including the factual findings and conclusions that justified terminating the investigation before OIG finalized its decision to close the complaint in 8 of the 9 complaints OIG investigated.[67] In addition, we found that OIG sent the complainant a final termination report when OIG terminated most of these investigations (7 of 8).[68] Further, OIG generally included information required under the regulations, such as a summary of relevant facts, OIG's reasons for terminating in the investigation, and a response to the complainant's comments, in these final termination reports.[69]

We found that OIG did not send a proposed termination report in any of the 27 complaints OIG declined to investigate, in accordance with OIG's interpretation of the regulations. In addition, although OIG sent a final termination report in most of the complaints (25 of 27, or 93 percent) OIG declined to investigate, OIG did not always include the reasons for its decision in the report. Specifically, we found that in 15 of the 24 final termination reports (63 percent) we reviewed for complaints OIG declined to investigate, OIG did not clearly explain the reasons for this decision.[70] Seven of these 15 reports indicated that OIG found that the complaint did not meet threshold regulatory requirements under the FBI whistleblower regulations, but the report did not communicate why. For example, in one instance, OIG's report to the complainant explained the general finding that the allegations, even if accepted as true, did not demonstrate a personnel action in retaliation for a protected disclosure. Information we reviewed elsewhere in this case file specified that OIG found that the complainant had not made the underlying disclosure to a designated entity under the regulations. However, OIG did not include this information in its final report to the complainant. In the 8 other complaints, OIG's final report to the complainant stated that another office should review the complaint, such as the FBI Inspections Division, but did not indicate the reason for this decision. In particular, the report did not indicate that OIG had considered the complaint as a whistleblower retaliation matter and determined the complaint did not meet threshold regulatory requirements for OIG to conduct an investigation.

In contrast, DOJ-OPR generally provided complainants proposed termination reports before closing their complaints and included required information in its final termination reports, including in complaints DOJ- OPR closed without conducting an investigation. Specifically, we found that DOJ-OPR sent a proposed termination report in 17 of 19 complaints (89 percent) that DOJ-OPR terminated, and included the office's findings and conclusions that justified terminating the investigation in all 17 of these reports.[71] In addition, we found that DOJ-OPR sent a final termination report in all 19 complaints and included relevant facts and the reasons for terminating the investigation in all 19 of these reports. Further, in all 9 complaints in which the complainant provided comments on the proposed termination report, DOJ-OPR responded to the complainant's comments in the final termination report.

Providing the complainant a proposed termination report describing the investigating office's findings and conclusions ensures that the complainant is aware of the office's rationale for the decision and has an opportunity to provide additional information or written comments before the office closes the complaint. According to two senior OSC officials we spoke with about their process for reviewing whistleblower retaliation complaints for most federal employees, OSC provides the complainant a letter when OSC intends to close a complaint that does not meet threshold requirements without conducting an investigation. In some instances, according to these officials, the complainant's response to OSC's proposed termination report has caused OSC to reconsider its initial decision to terminate the complaint. As with OIG and DOJ-OPR, if OSC intends to terminate a whistleblower retaliation investigation, OSC is required to provide the complainant a written statement including the facts and OSC's conclusions and provide the complainant an opportunity to provide comments. As previously discussed, OIG and DOJ-OPR are required to provide for the enforcement of whistleblower protection in a manner consistent with certain OSC processes.[72]

In addition, the requirement to provide specific information in the office's final report to the complainant, including the basis for the office's decision to close the complaint, helps ensure that complainants have the information they need to make decisions about their complaints. As discussed previously, the regulations provide complainants the option of bringing their complaints to OARM after the investigating office has notified them that it has closed the complaint.[73] However, without information on the reasons for OIG's decision to decline to investigate, complainants may not have sufficient information to determine if they would like to continue to pursue their complaints through OARM. Further, the regulations require complainants to bring their complaints to OARM within 60 days of receiving notification from the investigating office. If complainants need to request additional information from OIG, such as the rationale for OIG's decision, they may not have sufficient time to bring their complaints to OARM.

Senior OIG officials said that although they have not provided proposed termination reports in complaints they declined to investigate, they considered any additional information complainants provided after receiving notice of OIG's decision not to investigate. However, when we met with these officials in October 2014, they said that they recognize the benefits of always providing complainants the opportunity to comment on OIG's decision to terminate a complaint without initiating an investigation because the complaint does not meet threshold regulatory requirements. In addition, these officials said that they need to be more specific about the reasons a complaint does not meet regulatory requirements. In light of our review, these OIG officials said that they have decided to implement these practices and have instructed their investigators to do so going forward. We believe that, if implemented effectively, these planned actions will help OIG ensure that all complainants have an opportunity to provide additional information or written comments before OIG closes their complaints and that complainants will receive the information they need to make decisions about their complaints.

CONCLUSION

Whistleblowers play an important role in safeguarding the federal government against waste, fraud, and abuse, but they often risk retaliation from their employers as a result of their actions. DOJ has established a process by which FBI whistleblowers can seek recourse should they experience such retaliation, and DOJ generally has the discretion to revise this process, as needed. We found that DOJ has terminated many FBI whistleblower complaints based on complainants' failure to meet threshold regulatory requirements rather than whether the retaliation occurred. In particular, FBI employees are protected if they report wrongdoing to certain high-level FBI or DOJ officials and other specified entities, and—unlike employees of other executive branch agencies—are not protected if they report wrongdoing to their supervisors. DOJ officials have stated plans to partially address this by adding several more senior officials in FBI field offices to the list of individuals to whom complainants may report protected disclosures, but the timing and outcome of this stated plan are uncertain. DOJ officials said they do not plan to expand the list to include supervisors or others in an employee's chain of command in part because of their concerns about the additional resources that would be needed to handle a possible increase in complaints and the potential effect on the timeliness of DOJ's process to handle these complaints. While DOJ officials' concern about timeliness is important, they are already taking other steps to improve the efficiency of this process. More importantly, dismissing retaliation complaints made to an employee's supervisor or someone in that person's chain of command leaves some FBI whistleblowers with no recourse if they allege retaliation, as our review of case files demonstrated. Training that DOJ officials plan to provide to FBI employees could help provide information on how to make a protected disclosure; however, this planned training will not address the fact that some employees report alleged wrongdoing first to their supervisors or others in their chain of command without ever expecting that this will lead to retaliation and a whistleblower claim.

As a result, congressional consideration of whether the purposes of 5 U.S.C. § 2303, which prohibits a personnel action taken against an FBI employee as a reprisal for a protected disclosure, are being met—in particular, whether FBI employees should, like employees of other executive branch agencies, have a means to obtain corrective action for retaliation for disclosures of wrongdoing made to supervisors and others in the employees' chain of command—could help ensure that DOJ's process for handling these complaints is consistent with congressional action to strengthen and expand protections for other federal whistleblowers. Further, it is important that, regardless of what changes DOJ may make to the list of entities designated to receive protected disclosures, information DOJ and the FBI provide to FBI employees on the process for making a protected disclosure is clear and consistent so FBI employees who consult such guidance make decisions based on accurate information.

In some instances—particularly where OARM ordered corrective action in favor of the complainant—the process for resolving these complaints has taken many years, and DOJ has stated a commitment to improving its efficiency in handling these cases. Committing to specific time frames for returning DOJ decisions on the outcomes of FBI whistleblower retaliation cases could help DOJ achieve its commitment to improving efficiency in handling these complaints. Additionally, assessing the impacts of DOJ actions to improve timeliness could help ensure that these actions are achieving the intended results. Finally, establishing an oversight mechanism to monitor DOJ-OPR investigators' compliance with regulatory reporting requirements—either by tailoring DOJ-OPR's case management system or another means—can assist DOJ in ensuring that complainants receive timely information they need to make informed decisions regarding their complaints, such as whether or not to seek corrective action from OARM.

Matter for Congressional Consideration

To ensure that the purposes of 5 U.S.C. § 2303—which prohibits a personnel action taken against an FBI employee as a reprisal for a protected disclosure—are met, Congress may wish to consider whether FBI employees should have a means to obtain corrective action for retaliation for disclosures of wrongdoing made to supervisors and others in the employee's chain of command who are not already designated officials.

Recommendations for Executive Action

We recommend the following four actions.

To better ensure that FBI whistleblowers have access to recourse under DOJ's regulations should the individuals experience retaliation, and to minimize the possibility of discouraging future potential whistleblowers, we recommend that the Attorney General clarify in all current relevant DOJ guidance and communications, including FBI guidance and communications, to whom FBI employees may make protected disclosures and, further, explicitly state that employees will not have access to recourse if they experience retaliation for reporting alleged wrongdoing to someone not designated in DOJ's regulations.

To better ensure that DOJ is fulfilling its commitment to improving efficiency in handling these complaints, we recommend the following to the heads of the relevant offices:

- OARM and ODAG should provide parties with an estimated time frame for returning each decision, including whether the complaint meets threshold regulatory requirements, merits, and appeals. If the time frame shifts, OARM and ODAG should timely communicate a revised estimate to the parties.

- DOJ-OPR, OIG, OARM, and ODAG should jointly assess the impact of ongoing and planned efforts to reduce the duration of FBI whistleblower retaliation complaints throughout the entire investigation, adjudication, and appeal process to ensure that these changes are in fact shortening total complaint length, without sacrificing quality.

To ensure that complainants receive the periodic updates that they are entitled to and need to determine next steps for their complaint, such as whether or not to seek corrective action from OARM, we recommend that Counsel, DOJ-OPR tailor its new case management system or otherwise develop an oversight mechanism to capture information on the office's compliance with regulatory requirements and, further, use that information to monitor and identify opportunities to improve DOJ-OPR's compliance with regulatory requirements.

Agency Comments and Our Evaluation

We provided a draft of this report to DOJ and OIG for review and comment. On January 16, 2015, an official with DOJ's Justice Management Division sent us an email stating that the department concurred with our recommendations. DOJ also provided technical comments which we incorporated, as appropriate.

In its technical comments, DOJ stated a commitment to monitoring the implementation of its April 2014 recommendations to ensure that FBI employees are not unfairly excluded from whistleblower protection because they had disclosed information to their immediate supervisor. DOJ also reported that DOJ-OPR is taking steps, such as developing a report template and upgrading its case management system which, when completed, could help the agency begin systematically tracking investigators' compliance with regulatory reporting requirements. These initial steps position the agency to satisfy our recommendation that DOJ-OPR tailor its new case management system or otherwise develop an oversight mechanism to capture information on the office's compliance with regulatory reporting requirements.

In written comments provided by OIG, (reproduced in app. IV) the Inspector General concurred with our recommendation to OIG and provided technical comments which we incorporated, as appropriate. In its comment letter, OIG stated that OIG has consistently supported and continues to support broadening the list of persons to whom protected disclosures can be made. Further, with regard to guidance provided to FBI employees, the OIG fully supports providing clear and comprehensive guidance as to all aspects of whistleblower rights and protections.

To this end, OIG's letter stated that the office is working with the FBI to create a specialized training program that highlights the specific requirements and procedures for FBI whistleblowers and on enhancements to OIG's website to include additional information specific to FBI employees.

The OIG letter also raised several additional issues. First, OIG's letter stated that, with regard to the total duration of Jane Turner's complaint, for example, the GAO draft does not distinguish between the responsibilities of OIG and the department.

We appreciate the differing roles and responsibilities of each office and describe these in our report. In reporting our findings, we clearly distinguish between the separate offices' timeframes and records of compliance with certain regulatory requirements.

However, it is important for us to also consider the total length of cases, which is particularly important to the whistleblowers.

Second, the OIG letter mentioned that GAO's analysis excluded more recent complaints. Given the sensitive nature of open cases, we reviewed only complaints closed as of December 31, 2013.

Third, the OIG letter commented that the GAO report failed to fully acknowledge the high priority and personal attention OIG senior staff give to FBI whistleblower retaliation matters.

We disagree. Our report explains that the Inspector General personally reviews each complaint, but also recognizes that competing priorities for this high level of attention has resulted in delays. Fourth, OIG's letter noted that in many instances OIG has relied on telephone contact with complainants to meet regulatory notification requirements and because such contacts were not consistently documented, we would not always have identified them in our case file review.

In our review of both DOJ and OIG case files, we noted all evidence of contact with the complainants, including evidence of written and oral communication, but it is correct that we would not have identified undocumented contact with complainants.

As OIG acknowledged in its letter, it is important that evidence of contact be documented in case files to demonstrate compliance with the regulations. As discussed in our report, OIG has taken steps to address this.

Sincerely yours,

David C. Maurer
Director,
Homeland Security and Justice

APPENDIX I: SCOPE AND METHODOLOGY

This appendix discusses in detail our methodology for addressing the following three objectives:

- determining how long the Department of Justice (DOJ) has taken to resolve Federal Bureau of Investigation (FBI) whistleblower retaliation complaints and what factors have affected these time frames,
- determining the extent to which DOJ has taken steps to resolve complaints more quickly and determine the impact of any such efforts; and
- determining the extent to which DOJ's Office of the Inspector General (OIG) and Office of Professional Responsibility (DOJ-OPR) have complied with regulatory reporting requirements.

To determine how long DOJ has taken to resolve FBI whistleblower retaliation complaints and the factors that affected these time frames, we reviewed DOJ case files for all FBI whistleblower retaliation complaints closed within the last 5 calendar years (from 2009 through 2013). Specifically, we reviewed the case files for a total of 62 closed whistleblower retaliation complaints to calculate the duration of each complaint from initial filing to DOJ's final decision, including, for example, the length of time from initial filing to the investigating office's final decision; the length of time from filing a request for corrective action with the Office of Attorney Recruitment and Management (OARM) to OARM's decision; and the length of the appeals process.[74]

We did this by creating a data collection instrument to identify the key characteristics of whistleblower retaliation cases, determine the completeness of the files, and assess time frames for each case in accordance with DOJ's regulations.[75]

We also gathered information on the outcome of each complaint and factors that could affect timeliness, such as the length and frequency of parties' requests for extensions of time. In addition, to better understand DOJ's process for handling these complaints, we reviewed relevant documentation, including DOJ's whistleblower regulations and internal guidance on the process for making a protected disclosure. To obtain DOJ officials' perspectives on DOJ's process, time frames for handling these complaints, and factors affecting these time frames, we also interviewed senior agency officials from offices responsible for investigating—OIG and DOJ-OPR—or adjudicating—OARM and the Office of the Deputy Attorney General (ODAG)—FBI whistleblower retaliation complaints. We compared aspects of DOJ's process against standards in *Standards for Internal Control in the Federal Government* to identify the extent to which DOJ's process was in alignment with these standards.[76]

Because of the sensitivity of FBI whistleblowers' identities, to obtain whistleblower perspectives about DOJ's process and time frames, we met with representatives of whistleblower advocacy groups knowledgeable about DOJ's process and attorneys who have represented FBI whistleblowers through this process. Specifically, we identified and interviewed representatives of five whistleblower advocacy groups using an iterative process often referred to as snowball sampling. At each interview, we solicited names of additional groups to interview and selected for interviews those that were most widely recognized as knowledgeable about DOJ's process.[77] We also interviewed attorneys who had represented FBI whistleblowers in three of five cases where complainants have alleged retaliation and obtained corrective action.[78] These attorneys discussed their experience with DOJ's process and factors affecting the length of their cases. We analyzed the results of all of these interviews to distill themes and patterns. The information we gathered from these groups and attorneys—referred to throughout our report collectively as eight whistleblower advocates and attorneys—is not generalizable, but provides perspectives on whistleblowers' experiences with DOJ's process.[79]

To determine the extent to which DOJ has taken steps to resolve complaints more quickly, we interviewed senior DOJ officials in each of the four offices responsible for investigating or adjudicating whistleblower retaliation complaints—OIG, DOJ-OPR, OARM, and ODAG. We asked about the factors that affect the timely processing of these complaints and any efforts to address them.

In addition, to identify any practices that have improved timeliness in comparable federal settings, we interviewed senior officials in the Department of Defense's Office of the Inspector General as well as the U.S. Office of Special Counsel (OSC) and the U.S. Merit Systems Protection Board (MSPB)—federal agencies that handle whistleblower retaliation complaints for other federal employees—about those agencies' processes for handling whistleblower retaliation complaints. To identify the extent to which DOJ officials have taken steps to determine the impact of their efforts to improve timeliness, we interviewed DOJ officials and reviewed DOJ's April 2014 report to the President[80] and compared DOJ's stated plans with standards in *Standards for Internal Control in the Federal Government.*[81]

To determine the extent to which OIG and DOJ-OPR have complied with regulatory reporting requirements, we compared evidence we saw in DOJ's case files with DOJ's regulations and analyzed the extent of any discrepancies. Specifically, for each case file, we reviewed OIG's and DOJ-OPR's documented communications with the complainants, including initial and ongoing outreach, and recorded the dates of all communications in our data collection instrument.

We calculated the length of time between all documented communications to determine the number of complaints in which OIG and DOJ-OPR complied with the deadlines for reporting requirements in DOJ's regulations. In addition, we reviewed the content of the investigating office's final notice to the complainant that the office had closed its investigation or declined to open an investigation, as applicable, as well as the content of any interim notices stating the office's decision. We compared the content of these communications with DOJ's regulatory requirements. We also reviewed documentation and interviewed OIG and DOJ-OPR officials responsible for handling these complaints about any oversight mechanisms to ensure compliance with regulatory requirements. For example, we reviewed an electronic copy of an OIG spreadsheet for tracking regulatory deadlines for these complaints. We then compared these mechanisms against standards in *Standards for Internal Control in the Federal Government* to determine the extent to which OIG and DOJ-OPR met the relevant standards related to oversight.[82]

Further, we interviewed eight whistleblower advocates and attorneys, as noted above, to obtain whistleblower perspectives on the extent of DOJ's compliance with regulatory requirements and the effects of this compliance. In addition, because OSC serves a function comparable to those of OIG and DOJ- OPR in handling whistleblower complaints for most other executive branch employees and has similar regulatory reporting requirements, we interviewed OSC officials about OSC's processes and mechanisms for ensuring compliance with its requirements.

We conducted this performance audit from September 2013 to January 2015 in accordance with generally accepted government auditing standards. Those standards require that we plan and perform the audit to obtain sufficient, appropriate evidence to provide a reasonable basis for our findings and conclusions based on our audit objectives. We believe that the evidence obtained provides a reasonable basis for our findings and conclusions based on our audit objectives.

APPENDIX II: DEPARTMENT OF JUSTICE'S REASONS FOR CLOSING FEDERAL BUREAU OF INVESTIGATION WHISTLEBLOWER RETALIATION COMPLAINTS

This appendix provides information on the Department of Justice's (DOJ) reasons for closing the 62 Federal Bureau of Investigation (FBI) whistleblower retaliation complaints we reviewed. These 62 complaints represent the universe of FBI whistleblower retaliation complaints that were closed within the last 5 calendar years (from 2009 through 2013) by the final DOJ office to review the complaint.[83]

We reviewed case files at both of the offices responsible for investigating these complaints—the Office of the Inspector General (OIG) and the Office of Professional Responsibility (DOJ-OPR)—as well as at the office responsible for adjudicating these complaints—the Office of Attorney Recruitment and Management (OARM)—and identified the final outcome in each complaint.[84]

Table 1. Final Outcome in Federal Bureau of Investigation (FBI) Whistleblower Retaliation Complaints, by Final Department of Justice (DOJ) Office to Review Complaint and Length of Complaint

Final office to review complaint	Final outcome	Number of complaints closed in less than 1 year	Number of complaints closed after 1 year	Total number of complaints
Investigating office—Office of the Inspector General (OIG) or Office of Professional Responsibility (DOJ-OPR)	**Complaint did not meet threshold regulatory requirements.** The office found that the complaint did not meet threshold requirements under the FBI whistleblower regulations.	33	6[a]	**39[b]**
	No reasonable grounds. The office investigated at least one allegation made by the complainant and found that there were not reasonable grounds to believe that a personnel action had been taken in retaliation for a protected disclosure.	3	3	**6[c]**
	Complainant withdrew complaint	1	0	**1**
Total number of complaints closed by the investigating office		**37**	**9**	**46**
Adjudicating office—Office of Attorney Recruitment and Management (OARM)	**Complaint did not meet threshold regulatory requirements.** OARM found that the complaint did not meet threshold requirements for OARM to review the merits of the complaint under the FBI whistleblower regulations.	7	2	**9**

Final office to review complaint	Final outcome	Number of complaints closed in less than 1 year	Number of complaints closed after 1 year	Total number of complaints
	No reprisal found. OARM reviewed the merits of at least one allegation made by the complainant and found either that the protected disclosure was not a contributing factor in the personnel action, or that the FBI had demonstrated by clear and convincing evidence that it would have taken the same action in the absence of the disclosure.	0	1	**1**
	Complainant withdrew complaint	0	3[d]	**3**
	OARM found reprisal and ordered corrective action	0	3	**3**[e]
Total number of complaints closed by OARM		**7**	**9**[f]	**16**
Total number of complaints closed by DOJ		**44**	**16**	**62**

Source: GAO review of OIG, DOJ-OPR, and OARM case files. | GAO-15-112.

[a] In 1 of these complaints, OIG found that the complaint did not meet threshold requirements under the FBI whistleblower regulations but investigated the complaint under its preexisting authority.

[b] In most instances, the investigating office determined that the complaint did not meet threshold regulatory requirements based on initial information submitted by the complainant; however, in some instances, the investigating office made this determination after taking some investigative steps, such as interviewing the complainant or requesting additional information. We included those complaints in this category.

[c] Some complaints we reviewed included multiple disclosures or alleged acts of retaliation. In some instances, OIG or DOJ-OPR investigated one allegation but determined other aspects of the complaint did not meet threshold requirements. We included those complaints in this category.

[d] In 2 of these complaints, the complainants withdrew after OARM determined that the complaints met threshold regulatory requirements. In the third complaint, the complainant withdrew before OARM determined whether the complaint met threshold regulatory requirements.

[e] In all 3 of these complaints, an investigating office had previously reviewed and terminated the complaint because, among other reasons, there was sufficient evidence to conclude that the personnel action would have been taken absent the disclosure. However, in all 3 complaints, OARM determined that at least one personnel action had been taken in reprisal for a protected disclosure. Figure 3 shows the overall length of these complaints, including the length of each office's review.

[f] These 9 complaints were reviewed by an investigating office before being reviewed by OARM. The investigating office completed its review of 6 of the complaints in less than a year and exceeded 1 year in 3 of the complaints.

The DOJ office reviewing a whistleblower retaliation complaint may close the complaint before conducting an investigation (in the case of OIG and DOJ-OPR) or considering the merits of the complaint (in the case of OARM) if the office determines that the complaint does not meet threshold requirements under the FBI whistleblower regulations. If the investigating office finds that a complaint meets threshold regulatory requirements, the office will open an investigation to determine if there are reasonable grounds to believe that a personnel action had been taken or will be taken in retaliation for a protected disclosure.

If OARM first determines that a complaint meets threshold requirements, OARM adjudicates the complaint to determine whether the disclosure was a contributing factor in the personnel action based on a preponderance of the evidence and whether the FBI has demonstrated by clear and convincing evidence that it would have taken the same personnel action in the absence of such disclosure. If the complaint is substantiated and the FBI is unable to meet its burden of proof, OARM will order that the FBI take appropriate corrective action. In addition complainants may voluntarily withdraw their complaints. Table 1 summarizes the final outcome of the 62 complaints we reviewed, sorted by the final DOJ office to review the complaint and the overall length of the complaint.[85]

In addition to determining the final outcome in each complaint, we reviewed the case files to determine the reasons for the final DOJ office's decision to close the complaint.[86] For example, in some complaints, the final office determined that the complaint did not meet threshold regulatory requirements because the complainant's underlying disclosurehad been made to an individual or entity not designated in the regulationsand therefore the disclosure was not protected. In other complaints, the investigating office found that there were not reasonable grounds to believe the personnel action had been taken in reprisal for a protected disclosure because the evidence indicated that the personnel action would have been taken in the absence of the disclosure. Table 2 summarizes the reasons DOJ offices cited in their case files as reasons for closing whistleblower retaliation complaints and the number of complaints in which the final DOJ office to review the complaint cited each.[87]

Table 2. Reasons for the Department of Justice's (DOJ) Final Decision to Close Federal Bureau of Investigation (FBI) Whistleblower Retaliation Complaints

		Total number of complaints
One or more of the disclosures did not meet the definition of "protected disclosure" under 28 C.F.R. § 27.1(a).		**30**
	The complainant made the disclosure to an individual or entity not listed in the regulations.	23
	The disclosure did not evidence a violation of any law, rule, or regulation or other subject covered by the regulations.	7
	The complainant did not have a reasonable belief of wrongdoing when making the disclosure.	2
The complainant did not claim to have made a protected disclosure.		**1**
One or more of the alleged acts of retaliation did not meet the definition of "personnel action" under 28 C.F.R. § 27.2(b) or the complainant did not claim to have experienced a personnel action related to the disclosure.		**14**
The facts of the complaint did not demonstrate that the alleged retaliation had been taken in reprisal for the disclosure.		**16**
	The alleged retaliation occurred before the disclosure.	7

		Total number of complaints
	The timing of the personnel action was not reasonably close to the timing of the disclosure.	3
	The personnel action would have occurred had the complainant not made the disclosure.	6
	The evidence did not show that the alleged retaliator was aware of the disclosure.	4
	The evidence did not demonstrate a causal connection between the alleged retaliation and the disclosure.	2
	The complainant did not demonstrate that the disclosure was a contributing factor in the personnel action based on a preponderance of the evidence.	1
The complainant did not respond to requests for information necessary to show that the complaint met threshold regulatory requirements.		**3**
The complaint related to Equal Employment Opportunity (EEO) matters and should be addressed through that process.[a]		**7**
The allegations had previously been addressed by another office.		**1**
The complainant was not an FBI employee or applicant for employment with the FBI, as required by 28 C.F.R. § 27.1(a).		**2**

Table 2. (Continued)

		Total number of complaints
The complainant filed a request for corrective action with the Office of Attorney Recruitment and Management (OARM) before bringing the complaint to an investigating office, as required by 28 C.F.R. § 27.4(c)(1).		**3**
The complainant brought the complaint to OARM but did not file a request for corrective action.		**2**[b]
The case file did not provide sufficient information to determine the reason DOJ determined that one or more of the complainant's allegations did not meet threshold regulatory requirements.		**10**[c]

Source: GAO review of Office of the Inspector General (OIG), DOJ Office of Professional Responsibility (DOJ-OPR), and OARM case files. | GAO-15-112

Notes: This includes all reasons cited in the case files for complaints DOJ closed because the complaint did not meet threshold regulatory requirements, complaints the investigating office closed after finding no reasonable grounds, and complaints OARM closed after finding no reprisal. The number of reasons exceeds the number of complaints we reviewed because, in some complaints, the final DOJ office cited multiple reasons in its decision to close the complaint. For example, in some instances, the final office found that the complaint did not meet threshold regulatory requirements but also noted that the facts did not demonstrate that the alleged retaliation had been taken in reprisal. Similarly, because some complainants alleged multiple disclosures, in some instances the final DOJ office determined that one or more of the disclosures did not meet the definition of a protected disclosure but opened an investigation with regard to one or more disclosures that it determined were protected. We counted complaints under each reason cited within the case files.

[a] Federal law protects federal employees and job applicants from discrimination because of race, color, religion, sex, national origin, age (40 or older), disability, or genetic information. These laws also make it illegal to fire, demote, harass, or otherwise "retaliate" against applicants or employees because they filed a charge of discrimination, because they complained to their employer or other covered entity about discrimination on the job, or because they participated in an employment discrimination proceeding (such as an investigation or lawsuit). Federal employees who believe that they have been retaliated against for a protected activity may file a complaint with the Equal Employment Opportunity Commission for corrective action. DOJ-OPR and OARM officials told us that they generally do not have jurisdiction over complaints of EEO-related reprisal, while OIG officials told us they generally do not exercise jurisdiction over complaints of EEO-related reprisal.

[b] In one of these complaints, the complainant had previously submitted the complaint to an investigating office and the investigating office found that the complaint did not meet threshold regulatory requirements. The complainant then submitted a letter to OARM stating an intention to file a request for corrective action but did not respond to OARM's request for additional information required to file the request for corrective action. In the second complaint, the complainant e-mailed OARM but did not file a request for corrective action after OARM informed the complainant that the complaint must first be filed with an investigating office before the complainant can file such a request with OARM.

[c] In these 10 complaints, we were not able to determine a specific reason for the investigating office's finding that one or more of the complainant's allegations did not meet threshold requirements based on information contained in the case file. For example, in some of these complaints, the investigating office's final letter to the complainant stated that the matters were more appropriate for review by another office or agency, but the case file did not indicate the office's basis for this determination.

Appendix III: Department of Justice (DOJ) Investigating Offices' Compliance with Selected Reporting Requirements

Requirement	Percentage and number of complaints that met requirement, by investigating office	
	Office of the Inspector General (OIG)	Office of Professional Responsibility (DOJ-OPR)
Acknowledgment of complaint: The investigating office must notify the complainant that it has received the complaint and provide the name of a contact person within the office within 15 days of either OIG or DOJ-OPR receiving the complaint.	44 percent (16 of 36)[a,b]	19 percent (4 of 21)[a,b]
First status update: The investigating office must provide the complainant with the first status update within 90 calendar days of acknowledging receipt of the complaint.	82 percent (14 of 17)[c]	65 percent (13 of 20)[c]
Subsequent status updates: The investigating office must provide the complainant with a status update at least every 60 calendar days after the first status update.	33 percent (4 of 12)[c,d]	20 percent (3 of 15)[c,d]
Overall timeliness: The investigating office must determine within 240 days of receiving the complaint if there are reasonable grounds to believe whistleblower retaliation occurred, unless the complainant agrees to an extension.	84 percent (31 of 37)[e]	80 percent (16 of 20)[e]
Closed complaint within 240-days	81 percent (30 of 37)[e]	50 percent (10 of 20)[e,f]
Obtained complainant's approval for an extension	14 percent (1 of 7)[g]	60 percent (6 of 10)[g]

Source: GAO analysis of Department of Justice (DOJ) regulations and information contained in OIG and DOJ-OPR case files. | GAO-15-112

Notes: We determined whether the investigating office met each requirement based on information contained in the case file for each complaint. In some complaints, the office may have met the requirement but not retained documentation in the case file.

[a] This excludes 1 OIG complaint in which we could not determine the date of the first notice to the complainant from information contained in the case file. We counted all complaints in which the investigating office communicated with the complainant within 15 days of the date either OIG or DOJ- OPR received the

complaint as meeting this requirement, including 1 OIG complaint in which the communication was not written, as required by 28 C.F.R. § 27.3(c). In 14 of the 16 instances in which OIG communicated with the complainant within 15 days, the communication included the name or contact information of a specific OIG staff person. We could not determine from the case files for 2 complaints if OIG included a contact in its first notice to the complainant because the content of the communication was not contained in the case files. DOJ-OPR included the name of a specific DOJ- OPR staff person in its first notice to the complainant in all 4 complaints in which DOJ-OPR communicated with the complainant within 15 days.

[b] In 2 DOJ-OPR complaints and 1 OIG complaint we reviewed, the investigating office received the complaint from the other office after more than 15 days had passed, but provided notice to the complainant within 15 days of the date the investigating office received the complaint. In an additional 2 DOJ-OPR complaints, DOJ-OPR received the complaint from OIG within 15 days of the date OIG received the complaint and DOJ-OPR provided notice to the complainant within 15 days of the date DOJ-OPR received the complaint, although more than 15 days had passed since the date OIG received the complaint. Because in these 5 complaints, more than 15 days had passed since either office received the complaint before the investigating office sent the complainant notice, these 5 complaints did not comply with the regulatory requirement.

[c] This excludes complaints closed before the deadline for the notice or update.

[d] In 3 of the 8 OIG complaints and 5 of the 12 DOJ-OPR complaints in which we did not see evidence that the office communicated with the complainant every 60 days, as required, we identified only one period of more than 60 days in which the case file did not contain evidence of communication between the investigator and the complainant.

[e] We considered a complaint to have met the 240-day requirement if the investigating office provided the complainant a final termination report or otherwise closed the complaint within 240 days from the date the office received the complaint.

[f] In 1 DOJ-OPR complaint we reviewed, the complainant initially provided an incorrect address and DOJ-OPR sent both a proposed and final termination report to the incorrect address within 240 days, but closed the complaint after more than 240 days because of the time needed to obtain the correct address. We excluded that complaint from our analysis of the number of complaints that met this requirement.

[g] In 1 OIG complaint and 1 DOJ-OPR complaint, the case file did not contain documentation that the complainant agreed to an extension, but did contain evidence of ongoing communication between the complainant or complainant's attorney and the investigating office after the 240-day deadline. We counted these 2 complaints as meeting the requirement.

APPENDIX IV: COMMENTS FROM THE DEPARTMENT OF JUSTICE OFFICE OF THE INSPECTOR GENERAL

U.S. Department of Justice

Office of the Inspector General

January 9, 2015

David C. Maurer
Director, Homeland Security and Justice
United States Government Accountability Office

Re: GAO-15-112

Dear Mr. Maurer:

Thank you for the opportunity to comment on the draft Government Accountability Office (GAO) report entitled "WHISTLEBLOWER PROTECTION – Additional Actions Needed to Improve DOJ's Handling of FBI Retaliation Complaints." (Draft). GAO has represented to the Office of the Inspector General (OIG) that this letter will be attached in full to the final GAO report released to Congress and the public.

We want to first acknowledge the hard work and professionalism of the GAO investigators involved in this project. As an independent oversight entity, we fully understand the difficulty and value of this important work. The OIG strongly believes that whistleblowers perform a service to their agency and the public when they come forward with information about potential wrongdoing, and that they should never be subject to reprisal for doing so. We have and will continue to implement reforms, before, during, and as a result of this review, in order to continue to make every effort to improve our efforts in this important area. Whistleblower rights and protections have been one of my highest priorities since becoming Inspector General in 2012.

Overview:

The OIG is a statutorily independent entity within the Department of Justice and its role in the process for addressing FBI whistleblower retaliation complaints is discrete and separate from the roles of other DOJ components. Accordingly, as an independent entity, once our investigative responsibilities are complete and we submit our report to the Department, the OIG has no further role in the adjudication process. As such, it is important to distinguish between the investigative role of the OIG and the adjudicative role played by the Department in order not to leave any misimpression that the OIG has a continuing role in the process, or control over any delays that may occur after the conclusion of our investigation, which of course we do not.

For example, the GAO Draft begins by describing the Jane Turner case, which the Draft notes took over 10 years from investigation to final adjudication, as an example of the lengthy time it takes the DOJ to resolve some retaliation complaints. The Draft later repeatedly references the fact that the "DOJ" can take 10 or more years to resolve FBI retaliation cases. However, it is important to note that the OIG completed our draft report in the Turner case in a timely manner, within about 10 months from receiving the complaint. We are concerned that, in stressing the 10 years it took to ultimately resolve the Turner matter, the Draft does not adequately distinguish between the investigative role of the OIG, which was completed in a timely fashion, and that of other Department offices with roles in the process.

The OIG's role in processing FBI whistleblower retaliation complaints is prescribed by regulation and consists of receiving, reviewing, and, in appropriate cases, investigating complaints to determine whether there is a "reasonable basis" to conclude that a reprisal for a protected disclosure has occurred. Under the regulations, the OIG has no role in the adjudication phase of the process, which occurs before the Department's Office of Attorney Recruitment and Management (OARM), or in the appellate phase of the case involving the Office of the Deputy Attorney General (ODAG).

In the Turner case highlighted in the Draft, after the OIG as Conducting Office completed its investigation in a timely fashion of approximately 10 months, we provided a draft of our report to the complainant for her comments as required under the FBI whistleblower regulations. Turner responded by submitting 300 pages of comments, and then withdrew her complaint to the OIG before we could address the comments. As permitted under the FBI whistleblower regulations, she then filed her complaint with OARM. Those post-OIG proceedings consumed the great bulk of the 10 years GAO cites.[1] In sum, by not distinguishing between the OIG and the Department, we believe that the GAO Draft fails to acknowledge the OIG's strong and consistent record of timely

---

[1] The GAO noted one additional case out of the 62 complaints it examined where the matter took the Department more than 10 years to complete. (See Figure 2.) The OIG was not the investigating office in this other retaliation matter. The Draft identifies a third complaint that took over 8 years to resolve. (See Figures 2 and 3.) The OIG was the investigating office for this matter, and as shown in Figure 3 of the Draft, we completed our phase of the matter in approximately one year.

completion of its discrete responsibilities under the FBI whistleblower regulations, 28 C.F.R. Part 27.

The OIG is fully committed to furthering the rights and protections of whistleblowers throughout the Department of Justice. To advance this work, we have established a Whistleblower Ombudsperson Program, created at my direction shortly after my arrival as Inspector General and before such positions were required by the Whistleblower Protection Enhancement Act and going well beyond the requirements of that statute. To lead this program, I assigned a member of my Front Office staff, with whom I consult regularly regarding whistleblower issues. We helped to create and we continue to chair the government-wide working group of federal whistleblower ombudsmen established through the Council of the Inspectors General on Integrity and Efficiency. Within the past year, we found that there were reasonable grounds to believe that two individual FBI employees had suffered reprisal for making protected disclosures in connection with an ongoing OIG review, and we referred the results of our investigation to DOJ's Office of Attorney Recruitment and Management for adjudication, as we publicly reported in our "Review of the Organized Crime Drug Enforcement Task Forces Fusion Center" in March 2014.

While the OIG has always pursued FBI whistleblower matters with the utmost dedication and commitment, we have been making important improvements to our process for handling such matters since the initiation of our Whistleblower Ombudsperson Program in mid-2012, and we will continue to make every effort to improve our processes, including based upon recommendations from external sources such as this GAO review, as well as independent outreach we have done with leading whistleblower organizations. For example, we have determined that there are areas for potential improvement in our processing of these complaints, and we have taken concrete steps to effect such improvements. Specifically, although we have been providing notice to complainants when we receive and are reviewing their complaints, we believe that the OIG can improve its compliance with the regulatory requirement to provide a written notice to the complainant within 15 days of receiving the complaint indicating that the allegation has been received and identifying a point of contact. See 28 CFR § 27.3(c). Similarly, while our investigators regularly and routinely have communicated with complainants about the status of our investigations, such communications have most often been through telephone contacts. Accordingly, we have found room for improvement in documenting the periodic status notifications that we provide to complainants pursuant to 28 CFR § 27.3(e), and in documenting the agreement of complainants to extend the time for making our "reasonable grounds" determinations should investigations continue beyond 240 days from the receipt of the original complaint under 28 CFR § 27.3(f). And, even before the GAO review was complete, the OIG adopted oversight mechanisms to improve our performance on these important matters. We appreciate GAO's careful review of this important topic, and will continue to make every effort to perform and document our role in the process for reviewing reprisal claims in the best possible manner.

The OIG has a strong and consistent record of timely completion of its responsibilities with respect to FBI whistleblower retaliation complaints.

Our review of available data relating specifically to the OIG's performance of its discrete role in addressing FBI whistleblower retaliation complaints confirms that the OIG has a consistent record of timely completion of its responsibilities. The OIG has processed a total of 73 Whistleblower retaliation complaints that were received in the six years since January 1, 2009. Of these, the OIG closed 52 complaints without conducting an investigation, most commonly because an investigation would not be fruitful because the facts alleged in the complaint, if accepted as true, would not meet one of the requirements for establishing a prohibited reprisal for making a protected disclosure under the regulation.[2] The OIG completed investigations of 10 other complaints. In 2 cases, the complainant withdrew the complaint before the OIG completed its investigation. In 9 cases, the OIG's investigation was still underway as of December 31, 2014. The median time it took for the OIG to determine that a complaint should be closed without an investigation was 23 days.[3] The longest was 142 days. The median time for the OIG to complete an investigation (including writing a report of investigation or final termination report) was 363 days. The longest was 478 days. We are committed to continued improvement, but these numbers reflect the strong commitment of the OIG to complete its role as Conducting Office efficiently and expeditiously.

The methodology in the Draft report excluded many of the more recent complaints that were included in calculating the foregoing numbers. However, the Draft provided relevant data in a footnote confirming the success of the OIG

[2] GAO's Draft refers to this determination as a "failure to meet threshold regulatory requirements."

[3] The calculations in this paragraph exclude four complaints for which available records did not permit us to make a determination of their duration.

in completing its determinations in the investigation phase. The Draft states that the OIG closed 81 percent of its complaints within 240 days, with a median length of just 35 days.[4] (Draft at 28, fn. 65.) We believe that this record further confirms our ongoing efforts to expeditiously carry out our responsibilities.

Although we have worked to achieve significant success in completing the investigative phase in a timely fashion, the OIG has, as discussed above, identified opportunities for improving our processes before, during, and as a result of the GAO review. For example, we recognized that we could do better in processing initial complaints faster, including by ensuring that they are transmitted to the OIG's Oversight and Review Division more quickly for initial review, and by conducting those initial reviews within 1 or 2 days of receipt when possible. We took further action to improve the timeliness of investigations and reports by creating a specialized Access database and SharePoint Site to facilitate case tracking, and by adopting model report language to make report writing more efficient. These steps are referenced in the report, but we believe that they are highly significant in demonstrating our continuing proactive efforts to handling these matters appropriately.

The Draft report references, but fails to fully acknowledge the high priority and personal attention that my senior staff and I have given to FBI whistleblower retaliation matters. My senior staff and I are regularly and directly involved in the discussion of these matters, and I personally review and approve every declination decision, termination report, and report to OARM.[5] I firmly believe that any additional time required by such involvement is well spent to ensure that these important matters receive the attention and priority that they deserve. Moreover, my Whistleblower Ombudsperson and I have met personally with representatives of the leading nongovernmental organizations active on whistleblower issues to discuss in detail their views as to how we can best perform our role in the process and further the protection of whistleblowers within the Department.

---

[4] The GAO sample also included one OIG matter, initiated in 2005, that was not resolved in the OIG phase until January 2009. This matter was not taken to OARM. Although this particular case was clearly not resolved in a timely fashion, it is not remotely representative of the OIG's performance over the past 6 years.

[5] The Draft acknowledges that I personally review "each complaint." (Draft at 21.) This understates, however, the personal and substantial involvement of my senior staff and I in every aspect of the OIG's involvement in these matters.

<u>The OIG has taken steps to improve its documentation of required status updates and extension requests.</u>

The FBI whistleblower regulations require that the Conducting Office provide periodic status notifications and obtain the consent of the complainant to any extensions of the 240-day period for completion of the investigation. The regulations do not require that the updates or agreements be in writing. See 22 C.F.R. §§ 27.3(e) and (f). In practice, the OIG is typically in frequent telephone contact with complainants during the investigation. In many instances, the OIG has relied on these conversations to satisfy the notification requirement of the regulation and in obtaining complainants' consent to extensions. However, we have not consistently documented these communications in our case files. The finding in the Draft report that the OIG has not consistently met the statutory requirement to provide such status notifications (Draft at 27) is based entirely on a file review, and does not account for previously undocumented oral communications that our investigators regularly have with complainants.

As noted above, we have acknowledged that improvement in our documentation of contacts with complainants is necessary to demonstrate our compliance with the regulations, and as a means of ensuring such compliance. We have already taken steps to effectuate this. As the GAO acknowledged,

> [I]n July 2014, during the course of our review, an OIG manager informed staff responsible for the complaints of the importance of documenting status updates within case files to ensure documentation of OIG's compliance with regulatory requirements to update complainants within prescribed time frames. Further, over the last 2 years, OIG has developed a database it now uses as a management tool to oversee investigators' compliance with requirements for communicating with complainants. According to senior OIG officials we spoke with, OIG decided to develop this database to help ensure that OIG meets its regulatory requirements. OIG managers use the database to track dates of interim communication, such as status updates, and the database calculates regulatory deadlines for subsequent updates and for closing the complaint. In addition, according to senior OIG officials, managers can use the database to run reports, such as to see upcoming deadlines for all open complaints. Although it is too soon to tell how effective this database will be, if used consistently, this database could help OIG

managers ensure investigators communicate with complainants in accordance with regulatory requirements. (Draft at 30.)

The OIG can represent that these measures have substantially improved its documentation of status notifications and agreements for extensions.

The OIG has modified its procedures with respect to decisions not to initiate an investigation.

As noted above, many complaints submitted to the OIG do not require or call for the opening of an investigation because the facts alleged in the complaint, even if accepted as true, would not be sufficient to satisfy an essential element of a retaliation claim under the regulation.[6] The OIG has closed such complaints by means of brief declination letters, not more detailed termination reports, which are only required for matters we investigate.[7]

Nevertheless, in the interest of enhancing the transparency of our review process and giving whistleblowers the fullest possible opportunity to provide additional information that may be relevant to our determinations, the OIG has begun providing more detailed information in our declination letters identifying the deficiencies in their complaints, including identifying the specific element or elements of a claim of reprisal under the regulation that are absent based on our review of the initial complaint.

We also now inform the employee filing the complaint that we are providing them with 10 business days to submit any additional relevant information or comment on the OIG's initial determination prior to the OIG's declination of the complaint becoming final. We agree with GAO these changes in practice, which we believe go beyond the regulatory requirement, "will help OIG ensure that all complainants have an opportunity to provide additional information or written comments before OIG closes their complaints and that complainants will

---

6 For example, the complaint may fail to allege a "protected disclosure" because the subject matter is not within the scope of protected disclosures under the regulation or the disclosure was not made to one of the persons or offices designated in the regulation to receive such disclosures.

7 Under the FBI whistleblower regulation, a proposed termination report and final termination report is required "[i]f the Conducting Office terminates an investigation." See 28 C.F.R. §§ 27.3(g) and (h). Where no investigation has been initiated, the regulation does not require the issuance of a termination report, and the OIG instead issues a declination letter. The Draft states that the OIG failed to provide "proposed termination reports" to complainants in this situation (Draft at 33), however, no proposed termination reports were required because no investigations were opened.

receive the information they need to make decisions about their complaints." (Draft at 35.)

GAO Recommendations

Only one of the recommendations made by GAO in the Draft Report pertains specifically to the OIG. It recommends that OIG work with the other relevant DOJ component to jointly assess the impact of ongoing and planned efforts to reduce the time for resolving retaliation complaints. (Draft at 37.) The OIG concurs with this recommendation.[8]

The Draft addresses at length the list of designated recipients of protected disclosures, and recommends that the Department provide recourse to FBI employees "who experience for reporting alleged wrongdoing to someone not designated in DOJ's regulations." (Draft at 13-17 and 37.) The OIG has consistently supported and continues to support broadening the list of persons to whom protected disclosures can be made.[9] With regard to guidance to FBI employees on the question of whom a disclosure must be made in order to be protected, the OIG fully supports providing clear and comprehensive guidance as to all aspects of whistleblower rights and protections. The Draft mentions the video prepared through the OIG's Whistleblower Ombudsperson Program, which points out where the rules for FBI employees differ from those applicable to other DOJ employees, as well as the OIG's related ongoing work with the FBI to create a specialized training program that highlights the specific requirements and procedures for FBI whistleblowers. (Draft at 18, 19.) The OIG also has a dedicated "Whistleblower Protection" page on its website, available to FBI employees and others at http://www.justice.gov/oig/hotline/whistleblower-protection.htm, with a section on FBI Whistleblowers that we have enhanced to include additional links to the applicable regulation and other information specific to FBI employees.

8 Although it is not listed as a formal recommendation, the Draft report states at page 26 that "assessing the impact on timeliness and quality throughout the entire investigation, adjudication, and appeal process to determine the impact on total complaint processing time will require a joint effort among OIG, DOJ-OPR, OARM, and ODAG." We fully support the goal, but with the understanding that, as noted at the outset of this letter, the OIG is a statutorily independent entity within the Department of Justice and its role in the process for addressing FBI whistleblower retaliation complaints is discrete and separate from the roles of other Department components.

9 To the extent the summary findings at the outset of the Draft report suggest that there is discretion as to whether to pursue an allegation on this basis, that is not the case – as the body of the Draft explains, the regulation sets forth to whom protected disclosures may be made, and there is therefore no basis to pursue an investigation under the regulation for disclosures made to other persons.

Appendices

Footnote 82 of the Draft may create a misimpression that the OIG will not investigate a complaint under the FBI whistleblower regulations if the complainant submitted the complaint to the FBI Inspection Division rather than to the OIG. That is not the case. The OIG reviews all complaints received by the FBI Inspection Division. The OIG identifies any such complaint that may be cognizable under the FBI whistleblower regulations, and then forwards them for consideration to the appropriate OIG personnel to examine more closely. Although the regulations require that retaliation complaints be filed directly with the OIG or DOJ-OPR, the OIG nevertheless will conduct a retaliation investigation of a complaint referred to us from the FBI if the complaint alleges facts that, if accepted as true, would otherwise be sufficient to establish the elements of a retaliation claim under the regulations. The OIG was unable to investigate the 18 complaints mentioned in footnote 82 because they were legally deficient under the regulation (in that they did not meet "threshold requirements," in the terminology used in the Draft report), not because they were originally submitted to the FBI rather than to the OIG.

Thank you again for the opportunity to comment on the Draft report on this very important topic.

Sincerely,

Michael E. Horowitz
Inspector General

End Notes

[1] Whistleblower Protection For Federal Bureau of Investigation Employees, 63 Fed. Reg.62,937 (Nov. 10, 1998). DOJ initially issued these regulations as an interim rule effective upon publication in the *Federal Register*; however, DOJ invited postpromulgation comments that were addressed in a final rule issued in 1999. Whistleblower Protection For Federal Bureau of Investigation Employees, 64 Fed. Reg. 58,782 (Nov. 1, 1999) (codified as amended at 28 C.F.R. pts. 0, 27).

[2] GAO, *Standards for Internal Control in the Federal Government,*GAO/AIMD-00-21.3.1 (Washington, D.C.: Nov. 1, 1999). These standards define the minimum level of quality acceptable for internal control in government and provide the basis against which internal control is to be evaluated. Internal control refers to the plans, methods, and procedures used to achieve missions, goals, and objectives.

[3] The five whistleblower advocacy groups we interviewed were the American Civil Liberties Union, the Brennan Center for Justice at New York University School of Law, the Government Accountability Project, the National Whistleblowers Center, and the Project on

[49] GAO

[50] Of the remaining 58 complaints, 46 were closed by OIG or DOJ-OPR or withdrawn by the complainant at the investigation stage and 12 were closed by OARM or withdrawn by the complainant while pending at OARM, but before reaching the adjudication stage.

[51] DOJ's regulations specify that the DAG is the deciding official for review of OARM decisions, and there is no language allowing the DAG to delegate his or her decision- making authority to a designee. See Whistleblower Protection For Federal Bureau of Investigation Employees, 64 Fed. Reg. at 58782 (stating the language "(or a designee)" after "Deputy Attorney General" has been stricken because the department does not "believe that the authority of the Deputy Attorney General to conduct a review should be delegated").

[52] Nine of the 16 complaints we reviewed that were filed with OARM had at least 1 associated request for extension. These requests for extension of time were generally unopposed by the other party. We saw evidence that 6 of the 69 requests (9 percent) we reviewed were opposed. Officials in the FBI's Office of the General Counsel—the office that represents the FBI in FBI whistleblower retaliation cases—report treating these cases like any other employment cases, in terms of the level of FBI resources and number of requests for extension.

[53] In 15 complaints we reviewed, OARM made decisions on whether the complaints met threshold regulatory requirements. If we exclude the 2 complaints where the complainant never filed a request for corrective action, parties waited from 4 to 475 days for OARM to issue these decisions. In the 4 cases where OARM made merit decisions, parties waited from 151 to 598 days for OARM to issue its decisions. The DAG took nearly a year or more to make half (3 of 6) of the appeals decisions in the cases we reviewed. The DAG's fastest appeal decision was rendered in 12 days and the longest in 499 days. We calculated these wait times from the day of the last complainant or FBI action on the complaint to the time DOJ provided the relevant decision.

[54] Under 5 U.S.C. § 7701(i)(1), for appeals submitted to MSPB, MSPB is required to "establish and announce publicly the date by which it intends to complete action on the matter. Such date shall assure expeditious consideration of the appeal, consistent with the interests of fairness and other priorities of the [MSPB]. If [MSPB] fails to complete action on the appeal by the announced date, and the expected delay will exceed 30 days, [MSPB] shall publicly announce the new date by which it intends to complete action on the appeal."

[55] The Senate report accompanying the Civil Service Reform Act of 1978—which established this requirement for MSPB—explained that the Committee on Governmental Affairs had completed a study on delay in the regulatory process, which identified better agency management and planning as one of the prime ways regulatory delays could be reduced and, as a result, the committee "unanimously adopted a recommendation that agencies make greater use of deadlines as a way to help eliminate delay." In addition, the committee noted that "administrative delay of cases before [MSPB] is especially troublesome because it directly affects in significant ways employees who may not even have a job while the appeal is pending." S. Rep. No. 95-969, at 61 (1978).

[56] 10 U.S.C. § 1034(e)(3). This information must also be reported to the Secretary of Defense and the Secretary of the military department concerned (or to the Secretary of Homeland Security where applicable).

[57] In June 2012, DOJ stated in questions for the record for the Senate Committee on the Judiciary that "the Department . . . is committed to making every effort to improve the efficiency of the Department's adjudication of FBI whistleblower cases."

[58] GAO

[59] According to OARM officials, OARM initially provided written notice of the mediation program to all parties with whistleblower retaliation complaints pending before OARM, except for a select few in which OARM was in the process of finalizing a decision dismissing the complaint because it did not meet threshold regulatory requirements, or where the parties were already engaged in settlement discussions pertaining to an

outstanding issue related to the amount of corrective relief due to the complainant. These officials stated that OARM currently notifies all parties with complaints pending before OARM about this option and the mediation program is also available and being used by OIG and DOJ-OPR during the investigation stage.

[60] OARM officials report that since the part-time attorney joined the staff, the number of OARM issuances has increased from 39 in fiscal year 2013 to 90 issuances in fiscal year 2014. Issuances refer to decisions on whether complaints meet threshold regulatory requirements, final determinations, and more routine initial orders including orders to show cause, orders on motions for extensions of time, and others.

[61] GAO

[62] We reviewed 58 investigating office complaints—37 OIG complaints and 21 DOJ-OPR complaints. (In 4 of the 62 total complaints we reviewed, the complainant filed his or her complaint directly with OARM before filing with an investigating office; therefore we did not review investigating office case files associated with these complaints.) The number of complaints included in our analysis for each requirement may not total 58 because, in some instances, we were not able to determine whether a complaint met the requirement from the information contained in the case file or the investigating office closed the complaint before the deadline for the requirement. In these instances, we excluded the complaint from our analysis.

[63] In addition to letters informing the complainant of the status of the investigation, we counted as status updates all evidence of communication from the investigating office to the complainant, including evidence of phone calls, e-mails, and interviews with the complainant. Senior OIG officials and a DOJ-OPR official responsible for managing these complaints told us that they consider both letters and less formal communications, such as phone calls and e-mails, to be status updates under the regulations since they provide the complainant with information about the status of his or her complaint.

[64] We considered a complaint to have met the 240-day requirement if the investigating office provided the complainant a final termination report or otherwise closed the complaint within 240 days from the date the office received the complaint. In 1 DOJ-OPR complaint we reviewed, the complainant initially provided an incorrect address and DOJ- OPR sent both a proposed and final termination report to the incorrect address within 240 days, but closed the complaint after more than 240 days because of the time needed to obtain the correct address. We excluded that complaint from our analysis with regard to this requirement.

[65] OIG closed 30 of 37 complaints (81 percent) within 240 days, and DOJ-OPR closed 10 of 20 complaints (50 percent) within 240 days. We found that the median length of the 37 OIG complaints we reviewed was 35 days and the median length of the 20 DOJ-OPR complaints we reviewed was 281 days.

[66] GAO

[67] In addition to these 9 complaints, we reviewed 1 other complaint OIG investigated. Because the complainant withdrew the complaint before OIG determined whether to terminate the complaint, we excluded that complaint from our analysis.

[68] This excludes 1 complaint in which the complainant brought the complaint to OARM after receiving OIG's proposed termination report. In the 1 complaint in which OIG did not send a final termination report, OIG opened a separate investigation into additional allegations made by the complainant in comments on the proposed termination report.

[69] Specifically, we found that OIG included a summary of relevant facts and reasons for terminating the investigation in 6 of 7 final termination reports. OIG included a response to the complainant's comments in the final termination report for 5 of the 6 complaints in which the complainant provided comments on the proposed termination report. In the 1 complaint in which OIG did not address the complainant's comments in the final termination report, OIG wrote a separate letter responding to the comments. In 1 complaint, OIG did not provide the complainant a proposed termination report; therefore, the

complainant could not have provided comments in response to the proposed termination report.

[70] This excludes 1 complaint in which we could not determine if the final termination report included the reasons for closing the complaint because the case file did not include a copy of the report.

[71] In addition to these 19 complaints, we reviewed 2 other DOJ-OPR complaints. Because those 2 complainants went to OARM before DOJ-OPR determined whether to terminate the complaints, we excluded those 2 complaints from our analysis.

[72] In particular, pursuant to presidential delegation, DOJ is required to provide for the enforcement of the prohibition against personnel practices taken in retaliation for protected disclosures consistent with 5 U.S.C. § 1214, which governs OSC's authority to investigate allegations of prohibited personnel practices and make recommendations for corrective action, among other things. As DOJ explained in issuing its regulations, the investigating offices (OIG and DOJ-OPR) have been granted powers and functions that are consistent with those granted to OSC under section 1214.

[73] Officials with both OIG and OARM told us that OIG's decision not to investigate a complaint is sufficient for the complainant to have met the requirement to bring the complaint to an investigating office—either OIG or DOJ-OPR—before filing it with OARM.

[74] The regulations require that whistleblower retaliation complaints be filed directly with OIG or DOJ-OPR. However, OIG officials report that OIG will investigate a retaliation complaint referred by the FBI if the complaint is sufficient to establish the elements of a retaliation claim under the regulations. Therefore, in addition to these 62 complaints, we also reviewed case files for 18 complaints that OIG received from the FBI. OIG officials told us that OIG reviews all complaints submitted to the FBI to determine if any complaints submitted to the FBI fall under OIG's jurisdiction, such as complaints that appear to allege FBI whistleblower retaliation. Because these 18 complaints were not submitted directly to OIG or DOJ-OPR, as required by § 27.3(a)(1), and OIG did not investigate these complaints as whistleblower retaliation complaints (or the complaint was withdrawn by the complainant before OIG made a determination), we excluded these 18 complaints from our analysis.

[75] In 1998, DOJ issued regulations that set forth the process for FBI whistleblowers to report complaints of retaliation for their disclosures. Whistleblower Protection For Federal Bureau of Investigation Employees, 63 Fed. Reg. 62,937 (Nov. 10, 1998). DOJ initially issued these regulations as an interim rule effective upon publication in *the Federal Register*; however, DOJ invited postpromulgation comments that were addressed in a final rule issued in 1999. Whistleblower Protection For Federal Bureau of Investigation Employees, 64 Fed. Reg. 58,782 (Nov. 1, 1999) (codified as amended at 28 C.F.R. pts. 0, 27).

[76] GAO, *Standards for Internal Control in the Federal Government,* GAO/AIMD-00-21.3.1 (Washington, D.C.: Nov. 1, 1999). These standards define the minimum level of quality acceptable for internal control in government and provide the basis against which internal control is to be evaluated. Internal control refers to the plans, methods, and procedures used to achieve missions, goals, and objectives.

[77] The five whistleblower advocacy groups we interviewed were the American Civil Liberties Union, the Brennan Center for Justice at New York University School of Law, the Government Accountability Project, the National Whistleblowers Center, and the Project on Government Oversight.

[78] This includes all five closed cases in which DOJ ordered corrective action in favor of an FBI whistleblower since DOJ issued its regulations in 1998. In all of these cases, DOJ substantiated the complaint and ordered that the FBI take corrective action, such as providing the complainant back pay or restoring that person to a prior position. In one case, the complainant represented his/her self and so did not have an attorney and in another case we attempted to meet with the attorney numerous times but the attorney was unable to meet because of schedule conflicts.

[79] Two representatives of a whistleblower advocacy group also represented an FBI whistleblower who obtained corrective action. Therefore, the eight whistleblower advocates and attorneys referred to throughout our report include four representatives of whistleblower advocacy groups, two attorneys who represented FBI whistleblowers, and two attorneys who represent a whistleblower advocacy group and have also represented an FBI whistleblower who obtained corrective action.

[80] Presidential Policy Directive 19, dated October 10, 2012, required that within 180 days, DOJ report to the President on the efficacy of its regulations pertaining to FBI whistleblower retaliation and describe any proposed revisions to these regulations to increase their effectiveness. DOJ submitted the required report to the President in April 2014, a year after the due date.

[81] GAO

[82] GAO

[83] The regulations require that whistleblower retaliation complaints be filed directly with OIG or DOJ-OPR. However, OIG officials report that OIG will investigate a retaliation complaint referred by the FBI if the complaint is sufficient to establish the elements of a retaliation claim under the regulations. Therefore, in addition to these 62 complaints, we also reviewed case files for 18 complaints that OIG received from the FBI. OIG officials told us that OIG reviews all complaints submitted to the FBI to determine if any complaints submitted to the FBI fall under OIG's jurisdiction, such as complaints that appear to allege FBI whistleblower retaliation. Because these 18 complaints were not submitted directly to OIG or DOJ-OPR, as required by § 27.3(a)(1), and OIG did not investigate these complaints as whistleblower retaliation complaints (or the complaint was withdrawn by the complainant before OIG made a determination), we excluded these 18 complaints from our review.

[84] We also reviewed Office of the Deputy Attorney General (ODAG) case files for the 4 complaints that were appealed to that office. Because the Deputy Attorney General either upheld OARM's decision or returned the complaint to OARM for review, we determined that OARM made the final determination in each complaint and, therefore, we included OARM's final determination for complaints that were appealed.

[85] As discussed previously in this report, if the investigating office finds that there are reasonable grounds to believe that there had been retaliation for a protected disclosure, the office forwards its investigative report with any recommended actions to OARM for adjudication. In certain circumstances in which OIG or OPR has not found in the complainant's favor or has not completed its investigation, the complainant may go directly to OARM to request corrective action. We did not identify any complaints in which the investigating office found reasonable grounds; however, in 12 of the complaints we reviewed, the complainant brought the complaint to OARM directly after submitting the complaint to an investigating office. In these 12 complaints, we considered the reasons cited in OARM's case file as the final reasons for closing the complaint, although, in some instances, OARM's determination differed from the investigating office's determination.

[86] We did not assess whether the evidence in the case file supported the office's determination.

[87] In some instances, the office did not inform the complainant of the reasons it determined that the complaint did not meet threshold regulatory requirements, such as through a final report, but discussed its rationale elsewhere in the case file. We included in table 2 all reasons noted in the case file for the final office's determination, including reasons cited in internal documents as well as reasons communicated to the complainant.

In: Whistleblower Protection …
Editor: Evelyn Brooks
ISBN: 978-1-63483-147-5

Chapter 2

STATEMENT OF SENATOR CHUCK GRASSLEY, CHAIRMAN, SENATE JUDICIARY COMMITTEE. HEARING ON "WHISTLEBLOWER RETALIATION AT THE FBI: IMPROVING PROTECTIONS AND OVERSIGHT"*

Since Congress passed the Whistleblower Protection Act in 1989, I have been saying that whistleblowers are a very important part of Government operations. By exposing waste, fraud, and abuse, they help keep Government honest and efficient. But despite all of our hard work over 25 years ago, whistleblowers are still fired, demoted, discredited, and ostracized—all for doing their patriotic duty and telling the truth.

Today, we are going to focus on whistleblower retaliation at the FBI. Why? The FBI's whistleblower policies need special scrutiny because the legal protections for its employees are weaker than at any other agency. The FBI is not subject to the Whistleblower Protection Act. It has its own, special rules, and employees have no ability to appeal for an independent judgment outside the Justice Department.

---

* Citation Information: This is an edited, reformatted and augmented version of a statement presented March 4, 2015 before the Senate Judiciary Committee.

Back in 2012, President Obama issued a directive that established limited protections for whistleblowers in the intelligence community. He required the Department of Justice to report on how effective the FBI regulations actually are in protecting whistleblowers. The Department submitted that report in April 2014—a year late.

In May 2013, I also asked the Government Accountability Office to look into the Department's handling of FBI whistleblower complaints. That report was published last.

Unfortunately, the Justice Department failed to identify a witness from the Attorney General's or Deputy Attorney General's office to talk about its report and recommendations for reform.

The GAO and the Justice Department reports have several important findings in common. I'll mention just two of them now.

First, both reports recognize that, unlike every other federal agency, FBI employees are not protected from retaliation when they report wrongdoing to their direct supervisors. This makes me scratch my head. The FBI culture requires a deep respect for the chain of command. The FBI encourages employees to report wrongdoing to their supervisors and within the chain of command. But it does not tell them they will have no recourse if they experience retaliation for doing so.

It is not surprising that the Department found a significant portion of FBI whistleblower complaints have been rejected because the whistleblower blew the whistle to the "wrong person." Two of our witnesses today tried to disclose waste or wrongdoing only to be told that their whistleblowing was not protected under FBI rules. Mr. Kiper went to the Assistant Director of the Training Division. That was the most senior person in his office at Quantico and ranked higher at the FBI than a Special Agent in Charge. But that official is not listed in the FBI whistleblower regulations. Similarly, Special Agent Mike German tried to blow the whistle to the Special Agent in Charge as required under the rules. But, the FBI said it didn't count because the initial contact went through the Assistant Special Agent in Charge. So, the FBI's so-called whistleblower protections did not protect these whistleblowers simply because of a technicality.

Second, both the GAO and the Justice Department reports confirmed that the Department subjects FBI whistleblowers to delay after delay in these cases. It took the Department more than ten years to finally uphold Jane Turner's retaliation claim, after she was fired for reporting that FBI agents took "souvenirs" from Ground Zero after 9/11. It took more than nine years to resolve Robert Kobus' claim of retaliation for reporting time and attendance fraud—just in time for him to plan his retirement.

As we know, however, justice delayed is justice denied. And even after finally winning vindication, was anyone ever held accountable for the retaliation against these whistleblowers? Not that I'm aware of. If no one pays a price, then it will happen again.

In addition to the findings in these two reports, the FBI appears to be engaged in a pattern of stonewalling the Inspector General—including in two investigations of FBI whistleblower complaints. On February 3, the Inspector General reported to Congress that the FBI failed to comply with its legal obligation to provide timely access to all records requested. The FBI said that it needed to review the records before it decided whether to provide access to the Inspector General. It took four months from the initial request for the FBI to cough up the documents. That is not how the law is supposed to work.

It should not take months of negotiations and a notice to Congress for the Inspector General to get access to documents in FBI whistleblower cases. That doesn't instill much confidence in the Department's willingness or ability to protect whistleblowers. The FBI needs to commit to cooperating with independent oversight of its treatment of whistleblowers.

To conclude, I am pleased that the Department has made recommendations in its 2014 report to improve FBI whistleblower protections. Those recommendations are a start, but they do not go far enough. Last week's report from the Government Accountability Office made that clear. If every other law enforcement and intelligence agency can protect disclosures of waste, fraud, or abuse to a direct supervisor, then why can't the FBI? Whistleblowers should not have to fear retaliation for speaking up, and they should not have to wait a decade for relief. And, they should not have to rely on Congress to see justice done.

In: Whistleblower Protection …
Editor: Evelyn Brooks

ISBN: 978-1-63483-147-5

Chapter 3

TESTIMONY OF MICHAEL GERMAN, FELLOW, BRENNAN CENTER FOR JUSTICE AT NEW YORK UNIVERSITY LAW SCHOOL AND FORMER FBI SPECIAL AGENT. HEARING ON "WHISTLEBLOWER RETALIATION AT THE FBI: IMPROVING PROTECTIONS AND OVERSIGHT"*

Chairman Grassley, Ranking Member Leahy, and members of the Committee, thank you for inviting me to testify about improving protections for FBI whistleblowers. FBI and Justice Department officials often pay lip service to protecting whistleblowers, but the byzantine, protracted procedures they employ all but ensure that FBI employees who report misconduct will not be protected from retaliation. New reports by the Justice Department and Government Accountability Office (GAO) make clear that the current system isn't working.[1] But the incremental improvements the Justice Department proposes are inadequate, and would keep FBI employees trapped in a system with substandard protections. A legislative solution is necessary to finally give FBI employees the protection they deserve.

When Congress provided whistleblower protections to federal employees through the Civil Service Reform Act of 1978 and the Whistleblower

* This is an edited, reformatted and augmented version of testimony presented March 4, 2015 before the Senate Judiciary Committee.

Protection Act of 1989, it exempted the FBI and other intelligence agencies.[2] Instead, it required the Attorney General to establish regulations designed to provide FBI employees with a system of protection "consistent with" those provided by statute to other federal employees.[3] When the Justice Department finally promulgated such regulations in 1997, they failed to meet this standard.[4] By choosing not to protect the most common form of whistleblower complaints – those made to direct supervisors through the chain of command – the Justice Department regulations function more as a trap for the unwary rather than a shield of protection.

The regulations divide investigative responsibility over reprisal claims between the Justice Department Inspector General, the FBI Office of Professional Responsibility, and the FBI Inspection Division, which inserts ambiguity and delay into the process. Further, the regulations establish an adjudication process through the Justice Department Office of Attorney Recruitment and Management (OARM) that lacks the appropriate administrative law standards and transparency necessary to ensure due process. In practice, as the GAO report makes clear, FBI whistleblowers have little chance of being heard, much less receiving timely relief from reprisals, or corrective action to make them whole. The three cases GAO documented in which OARM ordered some corrective action for FBI whistleblowers took between eight and ten years to adjudicate – almost half of a typical agent's career.[5]

The costs, both fiscal and emotional, of such prolonged litigation against one's employer certainly dissuade many FBI employees from reporting internal misconduct. Many others who start the process ultimately withdraw their complaints, or cut their losses and settle at disadvantageous terms.

I know the toll exacted on whistleblowers because I resigned from the FBI after this system failed to protect me from retaliation for internally reporting a mismanaged terrorism investigation. I provided detailed accounts of what happened to me in previous testimony in the House of Representatives.[6] Today I would like to focus on how Congress can improve the chances of future FBI whistleblowers by giving them effective and enforceable rights to report wrongdoing to their supervisors, a timely, independent investigation of their complaint, effective administrative due process, and access to federal courts once they have exhausted administrative procedures.

Congress Must Ensure FBI Employees Are Protected for Chain of Command Disclosures and Disclosures to Congress

At his nomination hearing, FBI Director James Comey said whistleblowers were critical to a functioning democracy. He argued that "[f]olks have to feel free to raise their concerns, and if they are not addressed up their chain-of-command, to take them to an appropriate place."[7] This sounds good, but any agents who follow his advice would not be protected under the Justice Department regulations governing FBI whistleblowers. These regulations require FBI employees to bypass the normal chain of command and report misconduct only to a handful of high-level officials in order to receive protection. In the field, the lowest ranked official authorized to receive protected disclosures is a Special Agent in Charge (SAC).

I can't overstate how difficult it would be for an agent to break protocol and report directly to an SAC. I served as an FBI agent for 16 years, was assigned to three different field offices, and worked undercover investigations in at least three more. In all that time, I had no more than ten personal audiences with an SAC, none of which occurred at my request. If I asked for a meeting with the SAC, he or she would immediately call the Assistant Special Agent in Charge to find out what I wanted, who would then call my supervisor with the same question, who would then call me in to ask what the heck I thought I was doing. My experience as an FBI whistleblower demonstrates how difficult it is to follow these procedures, and how illusory the protections are in reality.

In 2002, I was assigned to the Atlanta Division, but was asked to work undercover in a Tampa counterterrorism investigation. As the operation began, I learned the informant in the case had illegally recorded a portion of a conversation between two subjects earlier in the investigation, imperiling any possible prosecution. When the Tampa supervisor refused to address the matter and told me to just "pretend it didn't happen," I felt duty bound to report it.

Luckily, I researched the proper procedure, and realized I should make the report to the Tampa SAC. But I also knew that failing to provide notice to my chain of command in Atlanta would cause problems for them, which would ultimately cause problems for me. So I called my supervisor to tell him I was going to call my ASAC, to tell him I was going to call the Tampa SAC to make a whistleblower report.

When I talked to my ASAC, however, he asked me to write the complaint in an email to him, which he would forward to the Tampa SAC. This seemed reasonable, especially because I had little confidence the Tampa SAC would take my call. The FBI would later argue, however, that by transmitting the complaint through my ASAC, I forfeited my right to be protected from the reprisals I faced for sending that email. My experience isn't unusual. The GAO and Justice Department reviews confirm that a significant portion of retaliation complaints are closed because the whistleblower reported to the wrong FBI official.[8]

The Justice Department argues that it doesn't need to amend its regulations to protect whistleblower reporting to direct supervisors because it has no evidence that FBI employees are inhibited from reporting because of the short list of authorized recipients.[9] But I provided the Justice Department review group a 2009 Inspector General survey that showed 42 percent of FBI agents said they didn't report all the misconduct they witnessed on the job.[10] Eighteen percent said they never reported such wrongdoing.[11] These statistics would be troubling for any government agency. But for our nation's premier law enforcement agency they are simply astonishing. Reasons for not reporting included fear of retaliation (16 percent), a belief the misconduct would not be punished (14 percent), and lack of managerial support for reporting misconduct (13 percent).[12] Tellingly, 85 percent of those surveyed said if they did report wrongdoing it would be to their direct supervisor.[13]

Compelling the Justice Department to protect whistleblower disclosures to supervisors is an essential reform necessary to ensure FBI employees will report internal waste, fraud, abuse, mismanagement, and illegality that might threaten both our security and our civil liberties. Likewise, explicitly protecting disclosures to Congress will ensure that FBI employees will feel comfortable providing their elected representatives with information necessary for them to satisfy their constitutional oversight obligations.

Congress Should Ensure FBI Whistleblowers Receive a Timely, Independent Investigation of Their Retaliation Complaints

The current Justice Department regulations give the Inspector General discretion to hand responsibility for whistleblower retaliation investigations back to the FBI Office of Professional Responsibility or the FBI Inspection

Division. A 2009 Inspector General audit of the FBI's disciplinary processes "found problems with the reporting of misconduct allegations, the adjudication of investigations, the appeals of disciplinary decisions, and the implementation of discipline that prevent us from concluding that the FBI's disciplinary system overall is consistent and reasonable."[14] FBI whistleblowers should not have to depend on inconsistent and unreasonable investigations of their complaints.

In my case, I gave the Inspector General and OPR a signed, sworn statement alleging retaliation in December 2002. In February 2003, I gave both offices a second sworn statement after learning Tampa managers falsely denied the meeting in question had been recorded. I again alleged retaliation. The Inspector General investigator advised me that OPR would take the lead, but that the Inspector General would reserve the right to initiate a new investigation once OPR was through. Then I was told the FBI Inspection Division had taken the investigation away from OPR, and was conducting interviews in Tampa. When the Inspectors interviewed me months later, they informed me that they investigated allegations made by the Tampa managers that I spent $50 without authorization, though they found this wasn't supported by the facts. In effect, the Inspectors had performed a retaliatory investigation against me on behalf of the Tampa managers involved in my complaint. I believe the only reason they told me they did this investigation was to warn me they would entertain even the pettiest allegations against me if I continued pursuing the whistleblower complaint. Finally, in December 2003 the Inspector General investigator told me the Inspectors found no wrongdoing and closed the case. The Inspection Division investigation was a whitewash that allowed the reprisals against me to continue and delayed action on my complaint for a year.

This is not to say Inspector General investigations of FBI whistleblower complaints are always timely, fair, and objective. This wasn't true in my case, or in several others I identified in previous testimony, and have learned of since. In my case the Inspector General did not begin an investigation in earnest until after I reported the matter to this committee, resigned from the FBI, and went public with my story. In January 2006, the Inspector General issued an unpublished report confirming FBI officials mismanaged the Tampa terrorism investigation and falsified records to hide their misconduct.[15] No one was held responsible for these offenses. The report also found the FBI retaliated against me, but this was a year and a half after I resigned from the FBI, more than three years after my initial complaint, and four years after the events took place. All intelligence and investigative opportunities posed by the original terrorism investigation were forfeited to protect the FBI and Justice Department from embarrassment.

Despite several problems with the Inspector General investigation of my case, which Chairman Grassley detailed in a 2006 letter, I was far better off *because* this investigation took place than I would have been if it had not.[16] This process should be improved, rather than abandoned. To his credit, Inspector General Michael Horowitz, who took office in 2012, has made FBI whistleblower issues a higher priority. He appointed Robert Storch, a member of his senior staff, as an official whistleblower ombudsperson assigned to ensure whistleblower cases are handled promptly.[17] Mr. Storch has held several meetings with whistleblower advocates, and his presence should add a level of accountability over these cases going forward. Fostering a strong working relationship with the ombudsperson may help the committee improve its oversight of these matters.

Congress Should Require the Justice Department to Utilize Administrative Law Judges and Procedures in Adjudicating Whistleblower Retaliation Complaints, Subject to Judicial Review

The Justice Department's regulatory process for adjudicating FBI whistleblower complaints is insufficient to meet its statutory requirements to provide relief "consistent with" the WPA. The Office of Attorney Recruitment and Management (OARM) simply is not an independent and impartial adjudicator, and its processes lack the transparency and regularity necessary to ensure due process. As the American Civil Liberties Union and the National Whistleblower Center argued in a 2013 briefing memo to the Attorney General, FBI whistleblowers should be afforded a full, on-the-record hearing before statutory Administrative Law Judges, and all proceedings should comply with Administrative Procedures Act (APA) standards.[18] Reasonable time periods for adjudication and rulings should be established. All decisions should be published, subject to redactions necessary to protect the privacy of claimants and witnesses, so that litigants have equal access to precedential opinions. The adjudication delays the GAO documented and the lack of transparency under the current regulatory procedures amount to an effective denial of due process for too many FBI whistleblowers.

The Justice Department may argue that providing APA procedures may be too resource intensive, but there is a simple solution to this problem. Easily more than half of the FBI workforce does not have access to sensitive national security information that would require a departure from the Office of Special Counsel (OSC) and Merit System Protections Board (MSPB) procedures afforded other federal employees, including those working for other federal law enforcement agencies and the Department of Homeland Security. Congress could mandate a system for the Justice Department to quickly vet FBI whistleblower claims and disseminate those without national security implications to the OSC and MSPB. This could significantly relieve the workload for the Justice Department's regulatory process, and could improve outcomes for a majority of FBI whistleblowers who do not need to be in a closed system.

Like other federal employees, all FBI whistleblowers should also have the right to go to federal court to enforce their rights once administrative appeals are exhausted. FBI employees reporting violations of their rights under Equal Employment Opportunity laws regularly adjudicate their cases in federal court without imperiling national security. There is no reason to believe federal courts couldn't take adequate measures to protect sensitive information during FBI whistleblower cases as well.

CONCERNS REGARDING THE JUSTICE DEPARTMENT'S PROPOSED AMENDMENTS TO FBI WHISTLEBLOWER REGULATIONS

While several of the Justice Department's proposed amendments to the FBI whistleblower regulations are welcome and may significantly improve outcomes for FBI employees reporting misconduct, a few raise concerns. For instance, giving OARM the power to sanction litigants who violate protective orders is unnecessary and potentially risky, given the lack of transparency and accountability over OARM decision-making in FBI whistleblower claims.[19] In a worst-case scenario, OARM sanctions against a litigant might even amount to an unlawful reprisal against a whistleblower seeking relief. Where litigants before OARM engage in misconduct related to OARM proceedings, OARM can simply refer the allegations to the appropriate disciplinary authority.

Likewise, Congress should examine closely the Justice Department's proposal to establish a mediated dispute resolution program for FBI whistleblower cases.[20] While exploring alternative dispute resolution options is always attractive, and may provide an avenue for addressing some whistleblowers' concerns, such positive outcomes require good faith that is too often absent in these cases. FBI officials should not need a mediator to tell them they shouldn't retaliate against FBI employees who conscientiously report waste, fraud, abuse, mismanagement or illegality within the Bureau. It is the law. If FBI and Justice Department leaders allow agency managers to ignore the law in favor of misplaced institutional loyalty, it is hard to imagine mediators can convince them to follow it. However, if combined with effective investigatory and adjudicatory reforms, a mediation process could afford all parties with an alternative to litigation. For mediation to work, FBI managers and employees must have confidence that the FBI whistleblower protection mechanisms are effective, timely, and accountable.

Without effective reforms, FBI whistleblowers would be at a distinct power disadvantage during dispute resolution, in that they have few enforceable rights and little chance of prevailing through the existing regulatory process. Whistleblowers who agree to mediated dispute resolution might feel compelled to accept less than they deserve, and less than they would receive in an adjudicatory system that fairly and vigorously enforced their rights. Such a procedure could simply add one more delay to the already long and drawn-out regulatory process, and could provide FBI officials the opportunity to probe the strength of the whistleblower's case and identify FBI employee witnesses who could then be targeted for reprisals themselves.

While these concerns might seem cynical, I experienced two years of sustained and collaborative retaliation that pushed me out of the FBI, despite a career of superior performance and an unblemished disciplinary record. High-level FBI officials who had nothing to do with the original complaint initiated adverse personnel actions against me because they heard I was a whistleblower. While a dispute resolution process that was subject to proper oversight and accountability would be worth consideration, Congress should be careful to ensure this isn't just another weak and time-consuming process within an already ineffective regulatory scheme.

CONCLUSION

I believe the Justice Department's review of its regulatory performance in FBI whistleblower matters provides a unique opportunity for Congress to act. For the first time, the Justice Department is acknowledging its procedures for investigating and adjudicating FBI whistleblower reprisal cases are not as effective as they should be, and need to be reformed. The GAO study adds substantial evidence to support this conclusion. The door is open for Congress to enact legislation that would codify reforms that will finally provide the protections that the hard-working and conscientious FBI employees deserve. Protecting FBI whistleblowers will help ensure the FBI remains as effective and accountable as it possible.

Finally, I would like to thank Chairman Grassley and Senator Leahy for their decades of support for whistleblowers of all kinds, and particularly for FBI employees who too often have nowhere else to turn to when they face retaliation for reporting waste, fraud, and abuse within the Bureau. I benefitted personally from that support when I came to the committee with a sordid tale of a mismanaged undercover terrorism investigation, potentially criminal attempts to cover it up, and the failure of the Inspector General to protect me from retaliation for having reported it. I wasn't able to provide the committee with a single FBI document to prove what I said was true, yet Chairman Grassley and Senator Leahy made television appearances saying they believed me, and vowed to investigate. I can't tell you how much I and my family appreciated that vote of confidence during a very difficult period. I also want to thank the finest investigator I know, Sen. Grassley's Chief Investigative Counsel Jason Foster. His empathy, professionalism, and diligence in seeking the truth have guided many whistleblowers through dangerous waters. I am proud to have worked with him over the last ten years.

End Notes

[1] See, DEP'T OF JUSTICE, DEPARTMENT OF JUSTICE REPORT ON REGULATIONS PROTECTING FBI WHISTLEBLOWERS (2014), [hereinafter Justice Department report] available at http://www.grassley.senate.gov/sites/default/files/judiciary/ upload/Whistle blowers%2C%2010-21- 14%2C%20DoJ%20Response%2C%20report%20to%20CEG%2C%20RW%20request%20for%20releas e%20of%20PPP19%20report.pdf, and, U.S. GOV'T ACCOUNTABILITY OFFICE, GAO-15-112, WHISTLEBLOWER PROTECTION: ADDITIONAL ACTIONS NEEDED TO IMPROVE DOJ'S HANDLING OF FBI

RETALIATION COMPLAINTS (2015), [hereinafter GAO report], available at http://www.gao.gov/products/GAO-15-112

[2] Pub. L. No. 95-454, §§ 1001, 202, 92 Stat. 1111, 1113-8, 1121-31 (codified as amended at 5 U.S.C. §§2301-2306).

[3] 5 U.S.C. §2303(c).

[4] 28 C.F.R. part 27. See also, Letter from Stephen M. Kohn and David K. Colapinto, National Whistleblower Center, and Michael German, American Civil Liberties Union, to Attorney General Eric Holder (Feb. 4, 2013), available at http://www.whistleblowers.org/ storage/whistleblowers/docs/BlogDocs/2013-02-04-memo-changestopart27.pdf.

[5] GAO report, p. 22 (only 3 of the 62 FBI whistleblower complaints the GAO reviewed resulted in an OARM order of corrective action).

[6] See, FBI Whistleblowers Hearing Before the Subcomm. On Crime, Terrorism and Homeland Security, H. Comm on the Judiciary, 110th Cong. (May 21, 2008)(written testimony of Michael German) available at: https://www.aclu.org/files/images/general/ asset_upload_ file419_35426.pdf; National Security Whistleblowers in the post-September 11th Era: Lost in the Labyrinth and Facing Subtle Retaliation Hearing Before the Subcomm. on National Security, Emerging Threats and International Relations, H. Comm. On Government Reform, 109th Cong. (Feb. 14, 2006)(written statement of Michael German), at http://www.gpo.gov/fdsys/pkg/CHRG109hhrg28171/html/CHRG-109hhrg28171.htm and, http://babel.hathitrust.org/cgi/pt?id=pur1.32754076775919;view=1up;seq=1.

[7] See, Carl Franzen, FBI director nominee calls whistleblowers 'critical element of functioning democracy,' THE VERGE, Jul. 9, 2013, at http://www.theverge.com/2013/7/9/4507094/fbi-director-nominee-comey-testifieswhistleblowers.

[8] GAO report, p. 12-14; Justice Department report, p.7.

[9] Justice Department report, p. 12-14.

[10] U.S. DEPARTMENT OF JUSTICE OFFICE OF THE INSPECTOR GENERAL EVALUATIONS AND INSPECTIONS DIVISION REVIEW OF THE FEDERAL BUREAU OF INVESTIGATION'S DISCIPLINARY SYSTEM, REPORT NO. I-2009-002, p. 188 (May 2009), available at http://www.justice.gov/oig/reports/ FBI/e0902/ final.pdf.

[11] Id.

[12] Id., p. 120.

[13] Id., p. 119.

[14] Id. p. xii.

[15] U.S. DEPARTMENT OF JUSTICE OFFICE OF THE INSPECTOR GENERAL REPORT OF INVESTIGATION INTO ALLEGATIONS OF SPECIAL AGENT MICHAEL GERMAN, Jan. 12, 2006, (on file with author).

[16] Letter from Senator Arlen Specter, Senator Patrick Leahy, and Senator Charles Grassley to Department of Justice Inspector General Glenn Fine (Feb. 3, 2006) (on file with author).

[17] U.S. DEPARTMENT OF JUSTICE OFFICE OF THE INSPECTOR GENERAL PRESS RELEASE, DOJ Inspector General Announces New Whistleblower Ombudsperson, (Aug. 8, 2012), available at http://www.justice.gov/oig/press/2012/2012 08 08.pdf

[18] Letter from Stephen M. Kohn and David K. Colapinto, National Whistleblower Center, and Michael German, American Civil Liberties Union, to Attorney General Eric Holder (Feb. 4, 2013), available at http://www.whistleblowers.org/storage/whistleblowers/ docs/BlogDocs/ 2013-02-04-memo-changestopart27.pdf.

[19] See, Justice Department report, p. 14.

[20] See, Justice Department report, p. 11.

In: Whistleblower Protection …
Editor: Evelyn Brooks
ISBN: 978-1-63483-147-5

Chapter 4

TESTIMONY OF STEPHEN M. KOHN, EXECUTIVE DIRECTOR, NATIONAL WHISTLEBLOWER CENTER. HEARING ON "WHISTLEBLOWER RETALIATION AT THE FBI: IMPROVING PROTECTIONS AND OVERSIGHT"*

Chairman Grassley, Senator Leahy, and Members of the Committee. The Department of Justice's program for protecting FBI whistleblowers is broken. My testimony will focus on the devastating impact caused by the prolonged delays in deciding these cases.

By way of background, since 1993 I have continuously represented FBI employees in whistleblower proceedings. My law firm filed the federal lawsuit that forced President Clinton in 1997 to order the Justice Department to implement the FBI protections contained in the Whistleblower Protection Act, resulting in the formation of the current OARM process.

I want to focus my remarks on the cases of three heroic Americans who faced prolonged retaliation at the FBI for reporting serious misconduct: Former Special Agents Jane Turner2 and Bassem Youssef3, and current FBI employee Robert Kobus.4 Together they have 86 years of exemplary FBI service protecting Americans.

* This is an edited, reformatted and augmented version of testimony presented March 4, 2015 before the Senate Judiciary Committee.

Although working in different FBI offices and on different programs, the whistleblower protection program failed them all.

Robert Kobus has worked in the New York Field Office for 34 years as an FBI operations manager. He is nearing retirement. His commitment to law enforcement is both professional and deeply personal. His sister was murdered by al---Qaeda on September 11, 2001.

Mr. Kobus reported budget and time card fraud in his office. It was a simple case, and fully documented. But retaliation was swift – the FBI stripped him of his duties and literally isolated him by assigning him to work as the only person on a vacant floor amongst 130 empty desks. The DOJ Office of Inspector General (OIG), after a thorough investigation, found that the FBI retaliated against Mr. Kobus and ordered corrective action. It should have ended there and Mr. Kobus should have been restored to his former duties no later than 2007.

Instead, for more than nine years the FBI spent our taxpayers' money frivolously fighting Mr. Kobus. In the end he won. But ask him about this "victory" and the 9--- year process he lived through waiting until December of 2014 to finally receive corrective action. The FBI's uncontrolled bullying tactics, which went on continuously while DOJ endlessly reviewed his very simple case, ruined Mr. Kobus' promising career.

Jane Turner's case is even worse. She was one of the first female agents in the FBI and once had a stellar career. However, after disclosing to the Inspector General that FBI agents had illegally stolen property (by taking souvenirs) from those who died in the 9/11 attacks, she was subjected to brutal retaliation, including downgraded performance because she "embarrassed the FBI," stripped of all investigatory duties and was completely isolated (to the point where agents explicitly stated they commenced bringing their guns into the office because Ms. Turner blew the whistle). While her whistleblower case was pending, Ms. Turner resigned from her job after being given a bogus Notice of Proposed Removal.

Ms. Turner filed a whistleblower complaint in 2002, but it languished for 11 years. She finally "won" her case, and the Notice of Proposed Removal was withdrawn. But this happened years after she met the mandatory retirement age. Because of the delays in her case, the relief she obtained did nothing to make her whole or properly correct the abuses she suffered.

Finally, there is Supervisory Special Agent Bassem Youssef. Before blowing the whistle he received the highly prestigious DCI award from the Director of Central Intelligence for his spectacular contributions in counterterrorism. He also served as the FBI's first legal attaché in Riyadh,

Saudi Arabia and in the 1990's he successfully infiltrated the terrorist organization now known as al---Qaeda.

His case has been pending before the DOJ for more than nine years, with no end in sight. The corrective action he sought from the FBI was simply to be assigned work on operational counterterrorism cases – an area Mr. Youssef was exceptionally qualified to perform. Although the DOJ Office of Professional Responsibility (OPR) investigated Mr. Youssef's whistleblower complaint and quickly ruled in his favor, ordering him reinstated to operational counterterrorism work, the FBI appealed, and the case remains pending.

Regardless of the ultimate outcome of his case, the OARM process failed. Mr. Youssef's request to utilize his unique skills to fight America's war on terror will never come to pass. This past September, frustrated and humiliated by the prolonged delays and with the continuous stigma whistleblowers face within the FBI, Mr. Youssef finally retired, one year from his mandatory retirement date. Given his background and skills, this was a major loss for all Americans.

The prolonged delays in processing these claims send a clear message to all FBI agents: Don't blow the whistle.

Thank you.

SUPPLEMENTAL WRITTEN TESTIMONY

A. Summary of Needed Reforms

1. The law should be amended to include protections for FBI employees who make disclosures to their supervisors and/or through their chain of command. Without such protections the majority of whistleblowers will not be protected. This recommendation is consistent with the recommendation made by the U.S. General Accounting Office, "Whistleblower Protection: Additional actions Needed to Improve DOJ's Handling of FBI Retaliation Complaints," GAO-15-112 (January 2015), p. 41. http://bit.ly/1M3lJw2
2. Strict time limits must be placed on the adjudicatory process. Currently, if the OIG or OPR does not conclude their investigation in a specific time period, and FBI employee has the right to immediately appeal his or her case to the Office of Attorney Recruitment and Management ("OARM"). This process is appropriate, and puts real

pressure on the OIG or OPR to issue timely decisions. A similar process, with real teeth, must be placed on the two adjudicatory offices with responsibility over the FBI Whistleblower Program: the OARM and Deputy Attorney General ("DAG"). We recommend the following:

A. The OARM shall issue its initial decision on the merits and any final decision on remedy within 12 months of the filing of an appeal, not including enlargements of time requested and obtained by the employee. The failure to meet these deadlines will give the employee the right to remove his or her case to U.S. District Court, and have t he case heard de novo in that forum.
B. The DAG shall issue the final order of the Department of Justice within six months of the filing of an appeal before the DAG, not including enlargements of time requested by the employee. The failure to meet these deadlines will give the employee the right to remove his or her case to U.S. District Court, and have the appeal heard de novo in that forum.

3. In order to clear up any ambiguity in the law, Congress should explicitly clarify the law in order to ensure that any final decision of the DAG is subject to judicial review pursuant to the Administrative Procedure Act. Under 5 U.S.C. § 706 this review would be limited to ensuring that the DAG did not abuse his discretion in issuing the final order, and that the Department of Justice's final order was not arbitrary, capricious or in violation of law. Without such review the DAG could issue final decisions that explicitly violate the law, and the whistleblower would have no avenue to correct that manifest injustice.
4. Other needed improvements in the law are set forth in the Joint Recommendations submitted to the Department of Justice by the American Civil Liberties Union and the National Whistleblower Center on February 4, 2013. A copy of these recommendations can be found at http://bit.ly/ChangesPart27.

B. Background to the Whistleblowers

Former Supervisory Special Agent Bassem Youssef: Background on Mr. Youssef's 27---year career at the FBI, his whistleblower allegations and extensive documentation regarding his concerns can be found at http://bit.ly/Bassem Youssef.

FBI Employee Robert Kobus: Background on Mr. Kobus's 34---year career at the FBI and copies of the OARM decision ruling in his favor can be found at http://bit.ly/Robert Kobus.

Former Special Agent Jane Turner: Background information on Jane Turner, her whistleblower allegations, the OIG report finding that her allegations had merit and information on the retaliation she faced can be found at http://bit.ly/Jane Turner.

End Notes

[1] Stephen M. Kohn serves pro bono as the Executive Director of the National Whistleblower Center (www.whistleblowers.org). He is a partner in the Washington, D.C. law firm of Kohn, Kohn & Colapinto, LLP (http://www.kkc.com) served in the 1980 s as the Director of Corporate Litigation for the Government Accountability Project. His ninth book on whistleblowing is, The Whistleblower's Handbook: A Stepby-Step Guide to Doing What's Right and Protecting Yourself (Lyons Press, 3rd edition, 2013). The Handbook retold, for the first time, the history behind America s first whistleblower law, enacted by the Continental Congress in 1778. For over thirty years Mr. Kohn has successfully represented whistleblowers, including FBI employees such as Dr. Frederic Whitehurst, Jane Turner, Robert Kobus and Bassem Youssef. He also represents numerous whistleblowers in tax, securities and government contracting fraud cases. The disclosures made by his clients have triggered over $15 billion in recoveries for the United States. Mr. Kohn has a B.S. in Social Education from Boston University, an M.A. in Political Science from Brown University and is a graduate of the Northeastern University School of Law.

[2] Detailed information on Jane Turner's case can be found at http://bit.ly/Jane Turner.

[3] Detailed information on Mr. Youssef's case can be found at http://bit.ly/Bassem Youssef.

[4] Detailed information on Mr. Kobus' case can be found at http://bit.ly/Robert Kobus.

In: Whistleblower Protection …
Editor: Evelyn Brooks

ISBN: 978-1-63483-147-5

Chapter 5

TESTIMONY OF J. RICHARD KIPER, SPECIAL AGENT, FEDERAL BUREAU OF INVESTIGATION. HEARING ON "WHISTLEBLOWER RETALIATION AT THE FBI: IMPROVING PROTECTIONS AND OVERSIGHT"*

Thank you, Chairman Grassley, Senator Leahy and other members of the Committee for holding this important hearing on Whistleblower Retaliation at the FBI. As a victim of unjustified adverse actions, I am grateful for the opportunity to share my experience with you.

Like thousands of other FBI employees, I work hard at my job every day. I have been rewarded for my efforts over the past 15 years – not only in terms of statistical accomplishments but I have also been honored with several incentive and recognition awards, including the Outstanding Law Enforcement Officer of the Year in the Southern District of Florida.

I take seriously my responsibility to keep the American people safe, but I also recognize the importance of effectively managing the resources they have entrusted to me. Whether it's helping to define the requirements for the FBI's new case management system or creating a database to manage human sources in Miami – I have always raised my hand when I believed FBI processes and products needed to be improved.

* This is an edited, reformatted and augmented version of testimony presented March 4, 2015 before the Senate Judiciary Committee.

However, I never imagined that my desire to promote excellence would be used against me.

In 2011 I accepted a position as Chief of the Investigative Training Unit at the FBI Academy. This was a position for which I was especially well-suited due to my investigative experience in the FBI, as well as my four degrees in education. At the FBI Academy, I continued to push for ethical and efficient solutions to problems, and I brought problems to the attention to the highest ranking leaders at the FBI Academy. Specifically, I brought to light the following issues:

1. Training Division's intentional misleading of the Office of Management and Budget (OMB) regarding the training of new agents and new analysts.
2. Training Division's wasteful decision to install SCION, the FBI's top secret computer system, in the Intelligence and Investigative Training Center building.

When I raised these issues with the Training Division leadership, I did not retain an attorney or study the Whistleblower statute to ensure I was making a disclosure of wrongdoing to "an appropriate recipient." I was just trying to do the right thing – as I've always done. I made these disclosures to the highest ranking officials at my work site, hoping these executives would at least consider making positive changes.

Instead, I was removed and demoted two GS levels.

The tool used to retaliate against me was the FBI's Loss of Effectiveness (LOE) process. From April 22 to May 3, 2013 an FBI Inspection team traveled to the FBI Academy to conduct an inspection. On the last day of inspection, Training Division executives told me I was being removed from my position as a result of a Loss of Effectiveness (LOE) finding. The news was shocking to me, as I had earned outstanding evaluations from my supervisors, enjoyed nearly-perfect climate survey results from my employees, and received four awards during my tenure at Training Division.

At the time I was told of my removal, the Training Division executives refused to tell me why I had received the LOE finding or why they had agreed with it. Five weeks after I was told of my removal, they finally provided to me the written justification for my LOE finding. Although the inspectors found absolutely nothing wrong with my unit, they documented several accusations against me that were demonstrably false. As Senator Grassley effectively articulated in a letter to Director Comey on September 26, 2014, the justification for my removal was "contradicted by the FBI's own documents."

It is worth noting that if I had been accused of actual wrongdoing – say driving under the influence, vandalism, or soliciting prostitutes – I would have been given a chance to challenge the investigation and appeal the adverse action. However, with the FBI's LOE process the accused have no avenue to appeal the findings, no chance to prevent the outcome, no recourse whatsoever.

In light of the irregular inspection practices and false statements used to justify my LOE finding, the only explanation for my removal and demotion is that of retaliation for having made the disclosures I mentioned earlier.

While no one in the FBI has disputed the fact that my LOE was based on false information, what they *are* contesting is that my Whistleblower disclosures were not *protected* because they were not made to a "qualifying individual" listed in 28 CFR 27.1(a). While conceding that my disclosures were made to the highest ranking official at the FBI Academy, the FBI insists the disclosures were not made to the "highest ranking official in any FBI field office" as the statute requires. According to this logic, the adverse actions taken against me could not have been taken in retaliation for my disclosures because my disclosures were not protected under the statute.

I have no doubt that my removal and demotion was retaliation for having made Whistleblower disclosures. I made these disclosures in good faith and I made them to the highest ranking officials at the FBI Academy, who outrank the "highest ranking official in any FBI field office."

Thank you for considering the expansion of the FBI Whistleblower protections so that the FBI is held accountable for its actions and held to the standard of its motto "Fidelity, Bravery, and Integrity."

Thank you again for holding this hearing and I would be happy to answer any questions you may have.

In: Whistleblower Protection …
Editor: Evelyn Brooks
ISBN: 978-1-63483-147-5

Chapter 6

STATEMENT OF KEVIN L. PERKINS, ASSOCIATE DEPUTY DIRECTOR, FEDERAL BUREAU OF INVESTIGATION. HEARING ON "WHISTLEBLOWER RETALIATION AT THE FBI: IMPROVING PROTECTIONS AND OVERSIGHT"*

Good morning Chairman Grassley, Ranking Member Leahy and Members of the committee. Thank you for the opportunity to appear before you today to discuss the issue of whistleblower retaliation within the FBI.

The FBI recognizes the important role played by whistleblowers in our law enforcement efforts. We take very seriously our responsibilities with regard to FBI employees who may protect disclosures under the regulations, and we appreciate this Committee's longstanding interest in these important matters. As Director Comey has told this Committee, "[W]histleblowers are ... a critical element of a functioning democracy." Employees "have to feel free to raise their concerns and if they are not addressed up their chain of command to take them to an appropriate place."

The FBI has taken considerable steps to assure that employees are aware of whistleblower protections and of the whistleblower process. The FBI along with the Department of Justice (DOJ) has worked and continues to work to improve the process and employee's education about the process.

---

* This is an edited, reformatted and augmented version of a statement presented March 4, 2015 before the Senate Judiciary Committee.

The Process for Making a Claim

All FBI whistleblowers are protected by federal law from retribution. Title 5, U.S.C. Section 2303 provides that:

> Any employee of the Federal Bureau of Investigation who has authority to take, direct others to take, recommend, or approve any personnel action, shall not, with respect to such authority, take or fail to take a personnel action with respect to any employee of the Bureau as a reprise for disclosure of information by the employee...which the employee or applicant reasonably believes evidences:
>
> 1. a violation of any law, rule or regulation, or
> 2. mismanagement, a gross waste of funds, an abuse of authority, or a substantial and specific danger to public health or safety.

The process for making a protected disclosure under the law specifies the set of persons to whom a disclosure of wrongdoing must be made in order to qualify as a protected disclosure. A disclosure may qualify as protected if it is made to the DOJ Office of Professional Responsibility (OPR), the DOJ Office of Inspector General (OIG), the FBI Office of Professional Responsibility (FBI OPR), the FBI Inspection Division (FBI–INSD) Internal Investigations Section (collectively, Receiving Offices), the Attorney General, the Deputy Attorney General, the Director of the FBI, the Deputy Director of the FBI, or to the highest ranking official in any FBI field office.

Any FBI employee who believes he or she has suffered a reprisal for making a protected disclosure may report the reprisal in writing to DOJ OPR or OIG. Some are also referred by the FBI Inspection Division to the OIG. OPR and OIG will then confer to determine which office will conduct an investigation into the alleged reprisal. The office that eventually conducts the investigation is known as the "Conducting Office." The Conducting Office investigates the allegation "to the extent necessary to determine whether there are reasonable grounds to believe that a reprisal has been or will be taken" for a protected disclosure.

As part of its investigation, the Conducting Office obtains relevant documents from the FBI and from any other relevant source, including the complainant. These documents may include, for example, e-mails and personnel files. The Conducting Office interviews witnesses with relevant knowledge, typically including the complainant, the person(s) who allegedly retaliated against the complainant, and others in a position to have knowledge of the relevant facts and circumstances.

If the Conducting Office finds that there is no reasonable basis to believe that a reprisal occurred, it provides a draft report to the complainant with factual findings and conclusions justifying termination of the investigation, and allows the complainant to submit a written response. Upon termination, the Office must so inform the complainant in writing, and must provide the reasons for termination, a summary of relevant facts ascertained by the Office, and a response to any written response submitted by the complainant.

If the Conducting Office determines that there are reasonable grounds to believe that there has been or will be a reprisal for a protected disclosure, it reports its conclusion, along with any findings and recommendations for corrective action, to the DOJ Office of Attorney Recruitment and Management (OARM).

Oversight and Review by Office of Attorney Recruitment and Management

In addition, any complainant may file a request for corrective action with OARM within 60 days of receipt of notification of termination of an investigation by the Conducting Office, or at any time beyond 120 days after filing a complaint with the Conducting Office if that Office has not notified the complainant that it will seek corrective action.

OARM's first step is to make a jurisdictional determination. To establish jurisdiction, a complainant must demonstrate exhaustion of Conducting Office remedies and allege in a non-frivolous manner that the complainant made a protected disclosure that was a contributing factor in the FBI's decision to take or not take (or threaten to take or not take) a personnel action against the complainant.

If OARM's jurisdiction is established, the parties then engage in discovery. OARM typically affords the parties 75 days to complete discovery, but extensions are often granted upon the parties' joint request. After discovery and any hearing, OARM sets a schedule for briefing on the merits, which typically takes two to four months to complete. OARM can grant corrective relief unless the FBI proves by clear and convincing evidence that it would have taken the same personnel action against the complainant even if he or she had not made the protected disclosure. After any merits hearing and filing of the parties' respective merits (or post-hearing) briefs, OARM renders a final determination on the merits.

Within 30 days of a final determination or corrective action order by OARM, either party may request review by the Deputy Attorney General (DAG) which typically involves another round of briefing. The DAG may set aside or modify OARM's actions, findings, or conclusions found to be arbitrary, capricious, an abuse of discretion, or otherwise not in accordance with law; obtained without procedures required by law, rule, or regulation having been followed; or unsupported by substantial evidence. The DAG has full discretion to review and modify corrective action ordered by OARM. However, if the DAG upholds a finding that there has been a reprisal, then the DAG must order appropriate corrective action.

PRESIDENTIAL REVIEW AND IMPROVEMENTS TO THE PROCESS

In response to Presidential Policy Directive (PPD) 19, DOJ undertook a review of the disposition of FBI whistleblower reprisal cases filed with OIG, OPR, OARM, and the DAG from the beginning of 2005 through March 15, 2014.

This review was conducted by a working group that included the Office of the DAG, the FBI, OARM, OIG, OPR, and the Justice Management Division. In addition, the Department consulted with the Office of Special Counsel and FBI employees, as required by PPD-19, as well as with representatives of non-governmental organizations that support whistleblowers' rights and with private counsel for whistleblowers. The co-chairs of advisory committee representing all FBI employees conveyed two main points, based upon their own prior consultation with various constituents. First, they stated that OARM takes too long to process cases. Second, the co-chairs stated that a better job could be done of making FBI employees conscious of the whistleblower process and its parameters.

Based on this review, DOJ proposed a number of legal, policy and regulatory steps that the Department believes may be warranted. DOJ and the FBI have started implementing many recommendations. Other recommendations require further development, including, where applicable, public notice and comment procedures involved in the rulemaking process. Recommendations that are currently being implemented include:

- *Providing access to alternative dispute resolution.* DOJ created a voluntary mediation program for FBI whistleblower cases. The program utilizes the DOJ Mediator Corps Program, which was created in 2009 to expedite and make more efficient the resolution of workplace disputes. Mediation is now available at all stages in the process at the request of the complainant.
- *Expanding resources for OARM.* Many have expressed concerns about the length of time it takes to adjudicate FBI whistleblower cases. With a consistent average of approximately ten new cases a year, the number of active FBI whistleblower cases on OARM's docket at any one time is relatively small. However, the pendency of several large, complex cases among the more routine cases, along with associated administrative responsibilities, significantly slows overall case processing times. Large, complex cases can slow the adjudicative process due to the multitude of procedural questions that may arise, requests to extend discovery, and extensive factual records that must be reviewed and analyzed after discovery has closed. A number of cases have taken several years to resolve; the longest case took ten years from the filing of the complaint with OIG to the final decision by the DAG. To address this issue, DOJ determined that OARM's resources should be expanded. In November 2013, OARM hired a part-time attorney to supplement the work of its full-time staff attorney. Since then, OARM has improved its case processing time.
- *Awarding compensatory damage.* In light of PPD-19, DOJ will amend its regulations to provide that OARM may award compensatory damages, in addition to other available relief.
- *Expanding the list of persons to whom a protected disclosure can be made.* DOJ recommends a limited expansion of the set of persons to whom a "protected disclosure" may be made. DOJ recommends expanding the persons to who protected disclosures may be made to include—in addition to the highest-ranking FBI field office official—the second-highest ranking tier of field office officials. This expansion would enhance the ability of employees to make protected disclosures within their own office. Such a change would mean that, in 53 field offices, a disclosure to the Special Agent in Charge (the highest-ranking official) or to any Assistant Special Agent in Charge (the second-highest ranking tier of officials, typically 2-3 per office) would be protected, assuming the disclosure's content qualified for

protection. In the remaining and largest three field offices – Los Angeles, New York City, and Washington, D.C. – a disclosure to the Assistant Director in Charge (the highest-ranking official) or to any Special Agent in Charge (the second-highest ranking tier of officials, typically 5-6 in these three offices) would be protected. DOJ will amend the regulations accordingly.

- *Improving training for FBI employees.* DOJ believes that it is essential that all FBI employees, as well as non-FBI employees involved in the DOJ's FBI whistleblower program, receive proper training on DOJ's regulations and the rights and responsibilities of all parties. The OIG Whistleblower Ombudsman, in connection with the FBI and other affected offices, is currently reviewing DOJ's training efforts regarding whistleblowing activities. As a result of this process, DOJ will implement a reinforced training program to ensure that (1) relevant employees receive appropriate training on a regular basis, and (2) that all employees are fully apprised of their rights and responsibilities.
- *Reporting findings of wrongdoing to the appropriate authority.* The whistleblower advocates recommended that any final decision that includes a finding of unlawful reprisal be forwarded to OIG, or other appropriate law enforcement authority, for consideration of whether disciplinary action is warranted against the officials responsible for the reprisal. OARM has recently implemented a policy of sending referrals to the FBI Office of Professional Responsibility, with a copy to the FBI Director. DOJ is amending its regulations to formalize this practice.
- *Providing authority to sanction violators.* DOJ supports revising its regulations to allow OARM to sanction litigants who violate protective orders. OARM would issue a protective order if necessary to protect from harassment a witness or other individual who testifies before it. Because OARM lacks sanction authority, there is currently no recourse available against a party who does not comply with a protective (or other) order, except for possible referral to a bar association. DOJ therefore will revise OARM's procedures or to propose revising its regulations, as appropriate, to include a provision providing sanction authority.
- *Expediting the OARM process through the use of acknowledgement and show cause orders.* At MSPB, within three business days of receipt of an appeal, an administrative judge issues an order which

acknowledges receipt of the appeal, and informs the parties of the MSPB's case processing procedures (e.g., pertaining to designating a representative, discovery, filing pleadings, the agency's response, settlement, etc.). In cases where there is an initial question about the MSPB's jurisdiction, the MSPB issues, along with the acknowledgment order, an order directing that the appellant show cause as to why the appeal should not be dismissed for lack of jurisdiction. The show cause order puts the parties on notice of the jurisdictional requirements and their respective burdens of proof. Although MSPB procedures do not apply to FBI whistleblowers, issuing similar orders in FBI whistleblower cases could increase the efficiency of case adjudication at the jurisdictional phase. Through the public notice and comment process the Department will propose modifying its procedures to more closely mirror the MSPB process.

- *Equalizing access to witnesses.* The whistleblower advocates who met with DOJ raised concerns about access to FBI witnesses. They noted that, in some cases, the FBI has been able to call former FBI management officials or employees as witnesses against the complainant, either through affidavits or testimony at a hearing. However, the complainant has been unable to compel the deposition of those witnesses because OARM lacks authority to compel attendance at a hearing of, or the production of documentary evidence from, persons not currently employed by DOJ. DOJ is considering whether to amend its regulations to prohibit a party from admitting affidavits into evidence from persons who are unavailable for cross-examination at a hearing or deposition, unless an access arrangement has otherwise been made.
- *Publishing decisions.* The whistleblower advocates recommended that decisions entered by OARM and the DAG be made available to the public, with appropriate redactions to protect the identities of employees and claimants. They suggested that publication of opinions would help potential whistleblowers provide information in a manner that would be protected and would assist them in litigating their cases should they suffer reprisal. Traditionally, these opinions have not been published due to the presence of law enforcement sensitive and Privacy Act-protected materials. DOJ is exploring whether it is possible to publish suitably redacted opinions in a manner that would provide useful information.

- *Publishing annual reports.* The whistleblower advocates recommended that DOJ publish the annual reports that the Attorney General submits to the President pursuant to a 1997 Presidential memorandum delegating to the Attorney General responsibilities concerning FBI employees under the Civil Service Reform Act of 1978, as amended by the Whistleblower Protection Act of 1989. The Department has previously disclosed the underlying data contained in the annual FBI whistleblower reports in response to congressional requests, and will publicly release this data annually in the future.

GAO Report on Additional Actions Needed to Improve DOJ's Handling of FBI Retaliation Complaints

We are also aware of the GAO's recent report on additional actions needed to improve DOJ's handling of FBI retaliation complaints. The FBI fully cooperated with the GAO's review and supports its recommendations, which were focused on DOJ's handling of claims of reprisal for making a protected disclosure. As noted above, DOJ has taken steps to improve their process for handling of retaliation claims.

Chairman Grassley, Ranking Member Leahy and Committee Members, I thank you for this opportunity to testify concerning whistleblower retaliation within the FBI. We take very seriously our responsibilities with regard to FBI employees who make protected disclosures under the regulations. Furthermore, we appreciate your interest in these matters. The FBI will not tolerate reprisals or intimidation by any FBI employee against those who make protected disclosures, nor tolerate attempts to prevent employees from making such disclosures. I am happy to answer any questions you might have.

In: Whistleblower Protection … ISBN: 978-1-63483-147-5
Editor: Evelyn Brooks

Chapter 7

STATEMENT OF MICHAEL E. HOROWITZ, INSPECTOR GENERAL, U.S. DEPARTMENT OF JUSTICE. HEARING ON "WHISTLEBLOWER RETALIATION AT THE FBI: IMPROVING PROTECTIONS AND OVERSIGHT"*

Mr. Chairman, Senator Leahy, and Members of the Committee:

Thank you for inviting me to testify today about how to improve protections for FBI whistleblowers and oversight of whistleblower retaliation matters. Whistleblowers perform an important service to their agency and the public when they come forward with information about potential wrongdoing, and they must never be subject to reprisal for doing so. We need to do all we can to foster and support a culture where Department employees are encouraged to report information they have about waste, fraud, abuse, and misconduct. In my tenure as Inspector General, I have seen first-hand how important whistleblower information is to our work. For these reasons, whistleblower rights and protections have been one of my highest priorities since becoming Inspector General in 2012.

To advance this work, we established a Whistleblower Ombudsperson Program, created at my direction shortly after my arrival as Inspector General

* This is an edited, reformatted and augmented version of a statement presented March 4, 2015 before the Senate Judiciary Committee.

– before such positions were required by the Whistleblower Protection Enhancement Act and going well beyond the requirements of that statute. To lead this program, I assigned a senior attorney from my Front Office staff, with whom I consult regularly regarding whistleblower issues. Our Whistleblower Ombudsperson created, with the help of Special Agent John Dodson, a video entitled "Reporting Wrongdoing: Whistleblowers and their Rights," which discusses whistleblower rights and protections applicable to all DOJ employees, and specifically points out where the rules for FBI employees differ from those applicable to others. The OIG is working with the FBI to create a specialized training program that highlights the specific requirements and procedures for FBI whistleblowers, and we also are providing training to employees of other Department components on these issues. The OIG also has a dedicated "Whistleblower Protection" page on its website, available to FBI employees and others at http://www.justice.gov/oig/hotline/whistleblower-protection.htm, with a section on FBI Whistleblowers that we have enhanced to include additional links to the applicable regulation and other information specific to FBI employees. We have reached out to the whistleblower community, so that we can hear from them first-hand about issues and challenges that concern them, and to ensure that they can provide us with constructive feedback on our work. And as a result of our internal training and education efforts, in the fall of 2013, the OIG was certified by the Office of Special Counsel pursuant to Title 5, United States Code, Section 2302(c).

In addition, we helped to create and we continue to chair the government-wide working group of federal whistleblower ombudspersons established through the Council of the Inspectors General on Integrity and Efficiency. In my capacity as Chairperson of the Council of IGs, I look forward to working with my fellow Inspectors General to enhance the prominence of whistleblower protection programs across the IG community.

I am proud of these efforts, and of the tremendous dedication of the OIG staff that handles these matters and cares so deeply about them. Nevertheless, like any organization, in order to continue to improve, we need to critically assess our efforts, and improve them as necessary. The OIG has implemented several reforms recently in order to improve the effectiveness and timeliness of our handling of our responsibilities under the FBI Whistleblower Regulations. And we very much appreciate the report of the Government Accountability Office (GAO). As an independent oversight entity, the OIG fully appreciates the difficulty of the GAO's work and value of its conclusions. We have and will continue to implement reforms, in our ongoing effort to improve our work in this important area.

Overview of the FBI Whistleblower Retaliation Regulations

The protection of civilian federal whistleblowers from reprisal began with the enactment of the Civil Service Reform Act of 1978 (CSRA), and was expanded by the Whistleblower Protection Act of 1989 (WPA) and the Whistleblower Protection Enhancement Act of 2012 (WPEA). These statutes generally make it illegal for federal agency supervisors to engage in an adverse personnel action against an employee in reprisal for revealing agency misconduct. While most federal employees can challenge alleged reprisals via the Office of Special Counsel and the Merit Systems Protection Board, Congress established separate procedures for FBI employees by providing for an administrative remedy within the Department of Justice. These procedures are contained in 28 CFR Part 27, known generally as the "FBI Whistleblower Regulations."

The FBI Whistleblower Regulations prohibit Department employees from taking or failing to take, or threatening to take or fail to take any personnel action against any FBI employee as a reprisal for making a protected disclosure. The regulations define a "protected disclosure" as information that the employee reasonably believes evidences (1) a violation of law, rule, or regulation; or (2) mismanagement, a gross waste of funds, an abuse of authority, or a substantial and specific danger to public health or safety. To be protected from being a source for reprisal under the regulations, the disclosure must be made to one or more of nine enumerated individuals or entities: the Attorney General, the Deputy Attorney General, the Director of the FBI, the Deputy Director of the FBI, the highest ranking official in any FBI field office, the OIG, the Department of Justice Office of Professional Responsibility (OPR), the FBI OPR, or the Internal Investigations Section of the FBI Inspection Division. A "personnel action" includes a decision about hiring, termination, promotion, transfer, pay or benefits, or any significant change in duties, responsibilities, or working conditions. If the complainant shows by a preponderance of the evidence that the protected disclosure was a contributing factor in the personnel action taken against him, the burden shifts to the agency to show by clear and convincing evidence that it would have taken the personnel action in the absence of the protected disclosure.

Role of the OIG as "Conducting Office"

The FBI Whistleblower Regulations establish a two-phase procedure for addressing allegations of illegal retaliation against FBI employees: an investigation phase and an adjudication phase. Either the OIG or the Department's OPR investigates, and the Department's Office of Attorney Recruitment and Management (OARM) adjudicates.

The process begins when an FBI employee or applicant who believes he or she has suffered an illegal reprisal submits a complaint, which the regulation indicates should be in writing, to either the OIG or OPR. The OIG and OPR consult to determine which of them will serve as the "Conducting Office" for the investigation phase. The Conducting Office begins by analyzing the complaint to determine whether it satisfies threshold regulatory requirements, including whether the facts alleged in the complaint, if accepted as true, would meet the requirements for establishing a prohibited reprisal for making a protected disclosure. If the complaint satisfies these threshold requirements, the Conducting Office commences an investigation to determine whether there are "reasonable grounds" to determine that a reprisal has been or will be taken for a protected disclosure. The regulations allow 240 days for the completion of this investigation, which may be extended with the agreement of the complainant. The investigation typically involves collecting and analyzing relevant documents, including e-mails, and interviewing the complainant and other witnesses with knowledge of relevant facts.

At the conclusion of the investigation, the Conducting Office prepares a draft report, which is provided to the complainant for comment. If the Conducting Office finds a reasonable basis to conclude that there has been or will be a prohibited reprisal, it reports that to OARM, which is responsible for adjudicating. If the Conducting Office does not find a reasonable basis to conclude that a reprisal has occurred, the complainant may nonetheless file a request for corrective action with OARM. (Alternatively, a complainant may file a complaint with OARM at any time 120 days after the complaint was filed with the OIG or OPR, even if the Conducting Office has not yet completed its investigation. In practice, however, complainants have rarely bypassed the investigation phase in this manner.)

The adjudication phase is a more formal, adversarial process to which both the complainant and the FBI are parties, the latter represented by the FBI's Office of General Counsel. The OIG, however, has no role in the adjudication phase or in any appeal of an OARM determination.

DATA REGARDING FBI WHISTLEBLOWER RETALIATION CASES PROCESSED BY THE OIG

In its capacity as the Conducting Office, the OIG has processed a total of 73 FBI whistleblower retaliation complaints that were received in the six years since January 1, 2009. Of these, the OIG closed 52 of the 73 complaints without conducting an investigation, usually because a complaint failed on its face to state a claim – which means that the facts alleged in the complaint, even if accepted as true, did not meet the regulatory requirements for establishing a prohibited reprisal. The OIG has completed investigations of 10 of the 73 complaints. With regard to 2 of the 73 complaints, the complainant withdrew the complaint before the OIG completed its investigation. And as to the remaining 9 complaints, the OIG's investigation was still underway as of December 31, 2014.

Our review of available data relating specifically to the OIG's performance of its discrete role in addressing FBI whistleblower retaliation complaints confirms that the OIG has a record of timely completion of its responsibilities. Since January 1, 2009, the median time it took for the OIG to determine that a complaint should be closed without an investigation was 23 days. The longest was 142 days. The median time for the OIG to complete an investigation (including writing a report of investigation or final termination report) was 363 days. The longest was 478 days. We are committed to continued improvement, but these numbers reflect the strong commitment of the OIG to complete its role as Conducting Office efficiently and expeditiously.

OIG EFFORTS TO IMPROVE THE FBI WHISTLEBLOWER RETALIATION PROCESS

The OIG is fully committed to furthering the rights and protections of whistleblowers throughout the Department of Justice. While we have always pursued FBI whistleblower matters with the utmost dedication and commitment, we have been making important improvements to our process for handling such matters, and we will continue to make every effort to improve our processes. These improvements have grown out of our own continual self-examination of our processes and recommendations from external sources such as the GAO's recent review of the Department's handling of FBI whistleblower retaliation complaints, as well as the independent outreach we have done with leading whistleblower organizations.

Since I became Inspector General in 2012, I have given high priority and personal attention to FBI whistleblower retaliation matters. My senior staff and I are regularly and directly involved in the discussion of these matters, and I personally review and approve every declination decision, termination report, and report to OARM. I firmly believe that any additional time required by such involvement is well spent to ensure that these important matters receive the attention and priority that they deserve.

We have determined that there are areas for potential improvement in our processing of these complaints, and we have taken concrete steps to implement such improvements. For example, we recognized that we could process initial complaints faster, by ensuring that they are transmitted to our Oversight and Review Division, which handles these matters within the OIG, more quickly for initial review, and by conducting those initial reviews within 1 or 2 days of receipt when possible. We also recognize that we can improve our compliance with the regulatory requirement to provide a written notice to the complainant within 15 days of receiving the complaint indicating that the allegation has been received and identifying a point of contact. Similarly, while our investigators regularly and routinely have communicated with complainants about the status of our investigations, such communications have most often been through telephone contacts. Accordingly, we have found room for improvement in documenting the periodic status notifications that we provide to complainants, and in documenting the agreement of complainants to extend the time for making our "reasonable grounds" determinations should investigations continue beyond 240 days, as provided in the regulations. We have used technology to assist our efforts to improve the timeliness of investigations and reports by creating a specialized Access database and SharePoint site to facilitate case tracking, and by adopting model report language to make report writing more efficient.

In addition, the OIG was an active participant in the Department's workgroup convened pursuant to Presidential Policy Directive/PPD-19, "Protecting Whistleblowers with Access to Classified Information." Among other things, PPD-19 required the Department to assess the efficacy of the FBI Whistleblower Regulations and to propose revisions to the regulations to increase their effectiveness. The Department's report, which was issued in April 2014, recommended several changes to policies and procedures to enhance the protection of FBI whistleblowers from retaliation. Among these proposals was the creation of a voluntary mediation program for FBI whistleblower cases. We believe that Alternative Dispute Resolution can focus the parties' attention at early stages of the dispute, providing a shortcut to resolution as an alternative to the sometimes lengthy and inefficient multi-phase procedures described above.

Another important change recommended by the Department was expanding the definition of persons to whom a "protected disclosure" can be made. Currently, a disclosure is protected if its content qualifies for protection and if it is made to one of the nine offices and officials designated in the FBI Whistleblower Regulations.

The Department recommended expanding this list to include the second-highest ranking official in any FBI field office (which is typically any of 2-3 Assistant Special Agents in Charge in the field office). The OIG endorses broadening the scope of the individuals to whom a protected disclosure may be made, which will provide FBI employees with a level of protection closer to that granted to most other civilian employees. In this regard, we note that a separate FBI policy, known as Policy Directive 0727, prohibits FBI supervisors from retaliating against an employee for raising a "compliance concern" to any supervisor in the employee's chain of command. This policy may offer broader protection than the FBI Whistleblower Regulations, but it is not enforceable through the procedures provided under those Regulations.

Lastly, the OIG has modified its procedures with respect to decisions not to initiate an investigation. As noted above, many complaints submitted to the OIG do not require or call for the opening of an investigation because the facts alleged in the complaint, even if accepted as true, would not be sufficient to satisfy an essential element of a retaliation claim under the regulation. The OIG has closed such complaints by means of brief declination letters, not more detailed reports. Nevertheless, in the interest of enhancing the transparency of our review process and giving whistleblowers the fullest possible opportunity to provide additional information that may be relevant to our determinations, the OIG is now providing more detailed information in our declination letters identifying the deficiencies in complaints, including identifying the specific element or elements of a claim of reprisal under the regulations that are absent and informing the employee filing the complaint that we are providing them with an opportunity to submit any additional relevant information or comment on the OIG's initial determination prior to the OIG's declination of the complaint becoming final. These changes in practice go beyond the regulatory requirements, and will help the OIG ensure that all complainants have an opportunity to provide additional information or written comments before OIG closes their complaints consistent with our desire to provide the maximum possible support for whistleblowers from the FBI and throughout the DOJ.

THE GAO REPORT

On February 23, 2015, the GAO released a report entitled "Whistleblower Protection – Additional Actions Needed to Improve DOJ's Handling of FBI Retaliation Complaints." The OIG reviewed a draft of the report in early January and submitted detailed comments on the report, which are attached as an Appendix to the final GAO report. We appreciate the GAO review, and believe that it made a number of useful observations regarding the procedures for resolving FBI whistleblower complaints, and recommendations for improvements with which the OIG agrees. We also share the GAO's concern about the length of the adjudicative process, including cases such as the one involving Jane Turner, which the report notes took over 10 years from investigation to final adjudication. As we noted previously, under the regulations, our role in the Department's process concludes once we finish our investigation, and we play no role in the adjudicative phase. Thus, in the Turner case for example, the OIG completed its draft report in a timely manner, within about 10 months from receiving the complaint, while the adjudicative phase (in which we had no role to play) lasted for 9 more years.

We fully support the goal of prompt resolution of whistleblower complaints, and look forward to continuing to improve our processes and to receive ideas and suggestions from all of the stakeholders in this critical area.

DOCUMENT ACCESS ISSUES IN FBI WHISTLEBLOWER RETALIATION CASES

I need to discuss another development that concerns me and that is hindering the OIG's ability to complete its FBI whistleblower retaliation investigations in a timely manner: the regular practice of the FBI of reviewing documents requested by the OIG in order to permit the FBI's Office of General Counsel (OGC) to determine whether they believe that the OIG is legally entitled to access them. In the context of FBI whistleblower retaliation cases, this raises two significant concerns.

First, having the FBI review documents that the OIG has requested in order to decide what records it should provide to the OIG regarding reprisal claims made against FBI supervisors creates, at a minimum, a significant appearance of a conflict of interest. This is particularly the case in light of the FBI OGC's direct involvement in the document review, given that in any subsequent adjudication of the whistleblower retaliation complaint before OARM, the very same FBI OGC will be responsible for defending the FBI and its managers against that claim of reprisal.

Second, these document reviews can seriously delay and impair our reviews. Most recently, this occurred in two FBI whistleblower retaliation investigations that are currently underway in the OIG. The document requests in issue were sent to the FBI on September 26, 2014, and October 29, 2014, respectively. After months of delays, the FBI finally produced most of the responsive e-mails to the OIG in February 2015. A major factor in the delays was the FBI's practice of reviewing e-mails requested by the OIG to determine whether they contain any information that the FBI maintains the OIG is not legally entitled to access, such as grand jury, Title III electronic surveillance, and Fair Credit Reporting Act information. The FBI has withheld materials from the OIG in these two whistleblowers cases following such a review, pending authorization from the Attorney General or Deputy Attorney General to produce the information to the OIG. However, Section 6(a) of the IG Act clearly provides that the OIG is authorized to have access to all records available to the agency relevant to the carrying out of our responsibilities, and it does not contain an express limitation of the OIG's access to these categories of information. Moreover, even if the Department's leadership were to authorize the FBI to give us such records, which it has consistently indicated it would do, a process allowing the OIG access to records of the Department only when granted permission by the Department's leadership is inconsistent with the OIG's independence and results in serious delays for our work.

Further, Section 218 of the Appropriations Act for Fiscal Year 2015 does not permit the use of funds appropriated to the Department to deny the OIG access to records in the custody of the Department unless in accordance with an express limitation of Section 6(a) of the IG Act. Section 6(a) does not expressly or otherwise limit the OIG's access to the categories of information that the FBI maintains it must review before providing records to the OIG. For this reason, on February 3, 2015, we reported the status of document production in these two FBI whistleblower matters to the Appropriations Committees in conformity with Section 218.

The FBI OGC's practice of delaying document productions to complete these unauthorized pre-production reviews threatens to compromise the ability of the OIG to complete its investigations within a timely fashion consistent with the FBI Whistleblower Retaliation Regulations. Department leadership chose to refer the FBI's interpretation of its OIG disclosure obligations to the Office of Legal Counsel (OLC) in May 2014. Although we were told by the Department last year that this was a priority, we are still waiting for that decision so that this unnecessary and wasteful impediment to our work can be removed, whether by OLC or otherwise. Every day that goes by without a decision results in a waste of FBI and OIG resources, in delays in the OIG uncovering waste, fraud, abuse, and mismanagement in its reviews and audits, and in harm to FBI whistleblowers who rely on the OIG to fully and fairly review their retaliation allegations in a timely manner. It is long past time to issue the OLC opinion so this dispute can finally be resolved.

Conclusion

Thank you again for the Committee's continued support for our Office and for our efforts to vigorously pursue the protection of whistleblowers, who perform an essential service to the Department and the public when they come forward with information about potential wrongdoing. I look forward to continuing to work closely with the Committee to ensure the OIG can continue to lead the effort to protect FBI and all DOJ whistleblowers from illegal retaliation. I would be pleased to answer any questions you may have.

In: Whistleblower Protection …
Editor: Evelyn Brooks

ISBN: 978-1-63483-147-5

Chapter 8

DEPARTMENT OF JUSTICE REPORT ON REGULATIONS PROTECTING FBI WHISTLEBLOWERS*

Department of Justice

The Honorable Charles E. Grassley
United States Senate Washington, DC 20510

The Honorable Ron Wyden
United States Senate Washington, DC 20510

Dear Senators Grassley and Wyden:

This responds to your letter of August 12, 2014, to the President, which requested a copy of the Attorney General's report titled "Department of Justice Report on Regulations Protecting FBI Whistleblowers." This report resulted from Presidential Policy Directive 19 (PPD-19), entitled "Protecting Whistleblowers with Access to Classified information." Your letter was referred to the Department of Justice (the Department) for response.

The Department recognizes the important role played by whistleblowers in our law enforcement efforts. We take very seriously our responsibilities with regard to FBI employees who make protected

* This is an edited, reformatted and augmented version of a report issued April 2014.

disclosures under the regulations. We appreciate your interest in these matters and, in response to your request, have enclosed a copy of the Attorney General's report. This report addresses the Department's process for handling and adjudicating FBI whistleblower complaints and for protecting whistleblowers from reprisal. Specifically, the report assesses the efficacy of the provisions contained in part 27 of title 28, Code of Federal Regulations, in deterring the personnel practices prohibited in section 2303 of title 5, United States Code, and in ensuring appropriate enforcement of that section.

To assess and recommend potential changes to the current FBI whistleblower process, the Department brought together key stakeholders to form a working group of attorneys from the Office of the Deputy Attorney General, the FBI, the Justice Management Division, the Office of Attorney Recruitment and Management (OARM), the Office of the Inspector General (01G), and the Office of Professional Responsibility (OPR). The working group analyzed and developed thoughtful suggestions for both streamlining and improving the process, to ensure that the FBI whistleblower procedures afford appropriate protections and that the process is a reasonably timely one. As part of its evaluation, the working group sought feedback from whistleblower advocates in the community, and the FBI consulted with its own employees - the ultimate beneficiaries of the Department's review. In addition, and pursuant to PPD-19, a draft of the report was circulated to the Office of Special Counsel for comment.

Based on this review, the report provides proposals and recommendations on a number of legal, policy, and regulatory matters, that the Department believes are warranted. As noted below, the Department has already started implementing some of these recommendations. Other recommendations will require further development, including, in some instances, the usual public notice and comment procedures involved in the rulemaking process. Specifically, the report proposes the following changes:

- *Providing access to alternative dispute resolution (ADR).* As a result of this review, the Department has created a voluntary mediation program for FBI whistleblower cases. This program utilizes the Department of Justice Mediator Corps Program, which was created in 2009 to expedite and make more efficient the resolution of workplace disputes. Mediation is available at all stages in the process at the request of the complainant. Through the notice and comment process, the Department will seek to formalize inclusion of the ADR program.

- *Awarding compensatory damages.* In accordance with PPD-19, the Department will propose amending its regulations to provide that OARM may award compensatory damages, in addition to other available relief.
- *Expanding the list of persons to whom a protected disclosure may be made.* Currently, a disclosure is protected 01) its content qualifies for protection, and (2) it was made to specific persons within FBI management. The Department supports expanding the list of people to whom protected disclosures may be made to include - in addition to the highest-ranking FBI field office official - the second-highest ranking tier of field office officials. Such a change would mean that, in 53 field offices, a disclosure to the Special Agent in Charge (the highest-ranking official) or to any Assistant Special Agent in Charge (the second-highest ranking tier of officials, typically 2-3 per office) would be protected, assuming the disclosure's content qualified for protection. In the remaining and largest three field offices - Los Angeles, New York City, and Washington. D.C. - a disclosure to the Assistant Director in Charge (the highest-ranking official) or to any Special Agent in Charge (the second-highest ranking tier of officials, typically 5-6 in these three offices) would be protected. The Department will propose amending the regulations accordingly.
- *Improving training for FBI employees. The* Department believes that it is essential that all FBI employees. as well as non-FBI employees involved in the Department's FBI whistleblower program. receive proper training on the Department's regulations and the rights and responsibilities of all parties. The OIG Whistleblower Ombudsman. in connection with the FBI and other affected offices. is currently reviewing the Department's training efforts regarding whistleblowing activities. As a result of this process, the Department will implement a new training program to ensure that (1) relevant employees receive appropriate training on a regular basis, and (2) that all employees are fully apprised of their rights and responsibilities.
- *Reporting findings of wrongdoing to the appropriate authority.* The Department. through OARM, has recently implemented a policy of referring any final decision that includes a finding **of** unlawful reprisal to the FBI Office of Professional Responsibility, and copying the FBI Director. The Department will propose amending the regulations to formalize this process.

- *Providing authority to sanction violators.* On several occasions, including in circumstances where the parties have requested the investigative file from OPR or 01G. the parties have agreed to enter a joint stipulated protective order to prevent the release of privacy-protected or sensitive law enforcement information. Currently, OARM does not have the authority to enforce such an order. To protect against the release of this sensitive information, the Department supports providing OARM with the authority to sanction those who violate protective orders similar to that provided to Merit System Protection Board (MSPB) administrative judges.
- *Expediting the OARM process through the use of acknowledgement and show cause orders.* At MSPB, within three business days of receipt of an appeal, an administrative judge issues an order which acknowledges receipt of the appeal, and informs the parties of the MSPB's case processing procedures (e.g.. pertaining to designating a representative. discovery. filing pleadings. the agency's response. settlement, etc.). In cases where there is an initial question about the MSPH's jurisdiction, the MSPB issues, along with the acknowledgment order, an order directing that the appellant show cause as to why the appeal should not be dismissed for lack of jurisdiction. The show cause order puts the parties on notice of the jurisdictional requirements and their respective burdens of proof. Although MSPB procedures do not apply to FBI whistleblowers, issuing similar orders in FBI whistleblower cases could increase the efficiency of case adjudication at the jurisdictional phase. Through the public notice and comment process the Department intends to propose modifying its procedures to more closely mirror the MSPB process.
- *Equalizing access to witnesses.* During the Department's review. whistleblower advocates who met with the Department raised concerns about access to FBI witnesses. They noted that, in some cases, the FBI has been able to call former FBI management officials or employees as witnesses against the complainant, either through affidavits or testimony at a hearing. However, they stated that the complainant has been unable to compel the deposition of those witnesses because OARM lacks authority to compel attendance at a hearing of, or the production of documentary evidence from, persons not currently employed by the Department. The Department will

consider whether to amend its regulations to prohibit a party from admitting affidavits into evidence from persons who are unavailable for cross-examination at a hearing or deposition, unless an equitable access arrangement has otherwise been made.

- *Expanding resources for OARM.* During the course of the Department's review, the Department determined that OARM's resources should be expanded to reduce the time necessary to adjudicate FBI whistleblower cases. In November 2013, OARM hired a part-time attorney to supplement the work of its full-time staff attorney. Since then. OARM has improved its case processing time.
- *Publishing decisions.* During the Department's review. whistleblower advocates recommended that decisions entered by OARM and the Deputy Attorney General be made available to the public, with appropriate redactions to protect the identities of employees and claimants. They suggested that publication of opinions would help potential whistleblowers better understand their rights and responsibilities and would assist whistleblowers in litigating their cases should they suffer reprisal. Generally, these decisions have not been published due to the presence of law enforcement-sensitive and Privacy Act-protected information. Often, OARM opinions are highly fact-dependent, with detailed personal information about the complainant inextricably interwoven into the legal analysis. To improve transparency in the process, the Department is exploring whether it is possible to publish suitably redacted opinions in a manner that would provide useful information to FBI employees and the public.
- *Publishing annual reports.* During the Department's review, whistleblower advocates recommended that the Department publish the annual reports that the Attorney General submits to the President pursuant to a 1997 Presidential memorandum delegating to the Attorney General responsibilities concerning FBI employees under the Civil Service Reform Act of 1978, as amended by the Whistleblower Protection Act of 1989. The Department has previously disclosed the underlying data contained in the annual FBI whistleblower reports in response.

We hope that this information is helpful. Please do not hesitate to contact this Office if we may provide additional assistance regarding this or any other matter.

Sincerely,

Peter J. Kadzik
Assistant Attorney General

Enclosure

cc: Hon. Patrick Leahy, Chairman, Senate Committee on the Judiciary
Hon. Orrin Hatch, Ranking Member, Senate Committee on Finance

DOJ REPORT ON REGULATIONS PROTECTING FBI WHISTLEBLOWERS

I. Introduction

The Department of Justice has prepared this report pursuant to Presidential Policy DirectivefPPD-19, "Protecting Whistleblowers with Access to Classified Information." The report:

> assesses the efficacy of the provisions contained in part 27 of title 28, Code of Federal Regulations in deterring the personnel practices prohibited in section 2303 of title 5, United States Code, and ensuring appropriate enforcement of that section, and describes any proposed revisions to the provisions contained in Part 27 of title 28 that would increase their effectiveness in fulfilling the purposes of section 2303 of title 5, United States Code.

PPD-19 at 5. Part II of this report provides historical context regarding the Department's efforts to protect Federal Bureau of Investigation (FBI) whistleblowers from reprisal. Part III explains the Department's current policies and procedures for adjudicating claims of reprisal against FBI whistleblowers. Part IV summarizes and analyzes statistics regarding the use of these policies and procedures in recent years. Part V describes how the Department has conducted this review, including consultations. Part VI discusses changes that the Department intends to make to its policies and procedures. Part VII discusses changes that have been proposed to the Department but that the Department believes are not warranted at this time.

II. Historical Background

The protection of civilian federal whistleblowers from reprisal began in 1978 with passage of the Civil Service Reform Act of 1978 (CSRA), and has been expanded legislatively via the Whistleblower Protection Act of 1989 (WPA) and the Whistleblower Protection Enhancement Act of 2012 (WPEA). Currently, federal employees fall into three categories. Most civilian federal employees are fully covered by the statutory regime and can challenge alleged reprisals via the Office of Special Counsel (OSC) and the Merit Systems Protection Board (MSPB). By contrast, some federal agencies that deal with intelligence are expressly excluded from the whistleblower protection scheme established by these statutes. The FBI is in an intermediate position; its employees are protected by regulations promulgated pursuant to the CSRA and WPA. *See* 28 C.F.R. Part 27. The regulations forbid reprisals against whistleblowers and provide an administrative remedy within the Department of Justice.

The CSRA set forth "prohibited personnel practices"—a range of personnel actions taken against federal employees for improper reasons. One such prohibited personnel practice is retaliating against an employee for revealing agency misconduct. Specifically, the CSRA made it illegal for an agency to

> take or fail to take a personnel action with respect to any employee or applicant for employment as a reprisal for
>
> (A) a disclosure of information by an employee or applicant which the employee or applicant reasonably believes evidences
>
> (i) a violation of any law, rule, or regulation, or
>
> (ii) mismanagement, a gross waste of funds, an abuse of authority, or a substantial and specific danger to public health or safety, if such disclosure is not specifically prohibited by law and if such information is not specifically required by Executive order to be kept secret in the interest of national defense or the conduct of foreign affairs.

Pub. L. 95-454 § 101(a) (codified at 5 U.S.C. § 2302(b)(8)). The CSRA created the MSPB and OSC to enforce the prohibitions on specified personnel practices.

The CSRA expressly excluded from this scheme the FBI, the Central Intelligence Agency, various intelligence elements of the Department of Defense, and, "as determined by the President, any Executive agency or unit thereof the principal function of which is the conduct of foreign intelligence or counterintelligence activities." Pub L. 95-454 § 101(a) (codified at 5 U.S.C. § 2302(a)(2)(C)(ii)).

For the FBI alone, the CSRA enacted a separate statutory provision that specifically prohibits reprisals against whistleblowers in its employment. As enacted, 5 U.S.C. § 2303 provided:

> (a) Any employee of the Federal Bureau of Investigation who has authority to take, direct others to take, recommend, or approve any personnel action, shall not, with respect to such authority, take or fail to take a personnel action with respect to any employee of the Bureau as a reprisal for a disclosure of information by the employee to the Attorney General (or an employee designated by the Attorney General for such purpose) which the employee or applicant reasonably believes evidences-
>
> 1) a violation of any law, rule, or regulation, or
> 2) mismanagement, a gross waste of funds, an abuse of authority, or a substantial and specific danger to public health or safety.
>
> For the purpose of this subsection, "personnel action" means any action described in clauses (i) through (x) of section 2302(a)(2XA) of this title with respect to an employee in, or applicant for, a position in the Bureau (other than a position of a confidential, policy-determining, policymaking, or policy-advocating character).
>
> (b) The Attorney General shall prescribe regulations to ensure that such a personnel action shall not be taken against an employee of the Bureau as a reprisal for any disclosure of information described in subsection (a) of this section.
>
> (c) The President shall provide for the enforcement of this section in a manner consistent with applicable provisions of section 1206 of this title.

Pub L. 95-454 § 101(a) (codified at 5 U.S.C. § 2303). In enacting section 2303, Congress provided protection to FBI employees only for disclosures made through limited internal channels—i.e., to the Attorney General or a designee. By contrast, the broader scheme applicable to most civil service employees that Congress created in section 2302 did not contain such restrictions on reporting.

In January 1980, the Department published a final rule implementing section 2303. The rule authorized the Department's Office of Professional Responsibility (OPR) to "request the Attorney General to stay any personnel action" against an FBI employee if the OPR Counsel determined that "there are reasonable grounds to believe that the personnel action was taken, or is to be taken, as a reprisal for a disclosure of information by the employee to the Attorney General (or a Department official designated by the Attorney General for such purpose) which the employee reasonably believed evidenced" wrongdoing covered by section 2303. 45 FR 27754, 27755.

Congress revisited these issues in the Whistleblower Protection Act of 1989, which significantly expanded the avenues available to most civilian federal employees. Among other things, the WPA allowed aggrieved employees to file an individual right of action alleging retaliation for protected disclosures—a vehicle that had not been available under the CSRA. The WPA amended section 2303 by replacing the requirement that the President "provide for the enforcement of this section in a manner consistent with applicable provisions of section 1206" with a requirement that enforcement be consistent with applicable provisions of newly-added sections 1214 and 1221. Sections 1214 and 1221 set forth the procedures under which OSC would investigate prohibited personnel practices and recommend or seek corrective action and the circumstances in which an individual right of action would be available.

The WPA also amended the regime generally applicable to civil service employees by revising section 2302 to protect only disclosures of "gross mismanagement," rather than disclosures of simple "mismanagement" as provided by the CSRA. The Senate Report explained the change to section 2302 as follows:

> While the Committee is concerned about improving the protection of whistleblowers, it is also concerned about the exhaustive administrative and judicial remedies provided under S. 508 that could be used by employees who have made disclosures of trivial matters. CSRA specifically established a de minimus *[sic]* standard for disclosures affecting the waste of funds by defining such disclosures as protected only if they involved "a gross waste of funds." Under S. 508, the Committee establishes a similar de minimus standard for disclosures of mismanagement by protecting them only if they involve "gross mismanagement."

S.Rep. No. 413, 100th Con. 2d Sess. at 13 (1988). However, for reasons not clear from the legislative record, the WPA did not make a corresponding change to section 2303. Thus, the law continued to cover FBI whistleblowers who disclosed "mismanagement," even if it did not rise to the level of "gross mismanagement."

In April 1997, President Clinton issued a memorandum to Attorney General Reno in which he delegated to the Attorney General the "functions concerning employees of the Federal Bureau of Investigation vested in the President by . section 2303(c)," and directed the Attorney General to establish "appropriate processes within the Department of Justice to carry out these functions." 62 FR 23123. The memorandum further instructed the Attorney General to provide to the President an annual report including the number of reprisal allegations received and their dispositions.'

In November 1999, the Department issued a final rule establishing procedures under which FBI employees or applicants for employment may make disclosures of wrongdoing. 64 FR 58782. The rule created a remedial scheme within the Department through which FBI employees could seek redress for having suffered reprisal for making a protected disclosure. Subject to minor amendments in 2001 and 2008, the rule remains in force.

III. Current Rule

A. *Definition of Protected Disclosure*

With regard to its content, a disclosure is protected only if (as under the 1980 final rule) the person making it reasonably believes that it evidences:

(1) A violation of any law, rule or regulation; or

(2) Mismanagement, a gross waste of funds, an abuse of authority, or a substantial and specific danger to public health or safety.

28 C.F.R. § 27.1(a).

Unlike the 1980 rule, which authorized disclosures to the Attorney General or designee, the current rule specifies the set of persons to whom a disclosure of wrongdoing must be made in order to qualify as a protected disclosure. A disclosure may qualify as protected only if it is made to

> the Department of Justice's (Department's) Office of Professional Responsibility (OPR). the Department's Office of Inspector General ((DIG), the FBI Office of Professional Responsibility (FBI OPR), the FBI Inspection Division (FBI-INSD) Internal Investigations Section (collectively, Receiving Offices), the Attorney General, the Deputy Attorney General, the Director of the FBI, the Deputy Director of the FBI, or to the highest ranking official in any FBI field office.

Id.

B. Investigation

An FBI employee or applicant who believes he or she has suffered a reprisal for making a protected disclosure may report the reprisal in writing to OPR or OIG (some are also referred by the FBI Inspection Division to the OIG). OPR and 010 will then confer to determine which office will conduct an investigation into the alleged reprisal. Occasionally, 01G **or** OPR may determine that one or the other component is more suited based on a variety of factors, including, for example, if one component has prior experience with the complainant, if the OIG has investigated the complainant for misconduct or is doing so at the time of the complaint, if the complainant alleges retaliation in connection with making a complaint to the OIG, or if the complainant's allegations are particularly relevant to the mission of the OIG. Otherwise, the offices typically will take turns. The office that eventually conducts the investigation is known as the "Conducting Office"; its role is roughly analogous to the role played by OSC for employees covered by section 2302. The Conducting Office investigates the allegation "to the extent necessary to determine whether there are reasonable grounds to believe that a reprisal has been or will be taken" for a protected disclosure. 28 C.F.R. § 27.3(d). The office has 240 days to make this determination unless granted an extension by the complainant. *Id.* § 27.3(0.

If the Conducting Office finds that there is no reasonable basis to believe that a reprisal occurred, it provides a draft report to the complainant with factual findings and conclusions justifying termination of the investigation, and allows the complainant to submit a written response. ***Id.*** § 27.3(g). Upon termination, the Office must so inform the complainant in writing, and must provide the reasons for termination, a summary of relevant facts ascertained by the Office, and a response to any written response submitted by the complainant. *Id.* § 27.3(h).

As part of its investigation, the Conducting Office obtains relevant documents from the FBI and from any other relevant source, including the complainant. These documents may include, for example, e-mails and personnel files. The Conducting Office interviews witnesses with relevant knowledge, typically including the complainant, the person(s) who allegedly retaliated against the complainant, and others (often other FBI employees working in the same unit) in a position to have knowledge of the relevant facts and circumstances.

If the Conducting Office determines that there are reasonable grounds to believe that there has been or will be a reprisal for a protected disclosure, it reports its conclusion, along with any findings and recommendations for corrective action, to the Department's Office of Attorney Recruitment and Management (OARM). *Id.* § 27.4(a). Alternatively, a complainant may file a request for corrective action with OARM within 60 days of receipt of notification of termination of an investigation by the Conducting Office, or at any time beyond 120 days after filing a complaint with the Conducting Office if that Office has not notified the complainant that it will seek corrective action. *Id.* § 27.4(c)(1).

The regulations limit the extent to which proceedings before the Conducting Office are admissible before OARM. Without the complainant's consent, a determination by the Conducting Office that there are reasonable grounds to believe a reprisal has been or will be taken may not be cited or referred to. ***Id.*** § 27.4(a). (Where the Conducting Office finds in favor of the complainant on some, but not all claims, the complainant might not consent to the report being cited or referred to in proceedings before OARM, in order to prevent OARM from seeing any negative findings.) Nor may the Conducting Office's written statement explaining the termination of an investigation be admitted unless the complainant consents. *Id.* § 27.3(i).

C. Adjudication

OARM's adjudicatory role is roughly analogous to the role played by the MSPB in cases arising under section 2302. OARM's first step is to make a jurisdictional determination. To establish jurisdiction. a complainant must (1) demonstrate exhaustion of Conducting Office remedies and (2) allege in a non-frivolous manner that the complainant made a protected disclosure under 28 C.F.R. § 27.1(a) that was a contributing factor in the FBI's decision to take or not take (or threaten to take or not take) a personnel action covered by 28 C.F.R. § 27.2(b) against the complainant.

If OARM's jurisdiction is established. the parties then engage in discovery. In the past, OARM would sometimes stay proceedings in a case for an extended period of time at the parties' request to pursue related claims in another venue or to pursue settlement. In 2011, OARM implemented new case processing procedures under which it will dismiss a claim without prejudice where the parties need additional time to engage in discovery, to pursue settlement, or to litigate claims in an alternate forum.

OARM typically affords the parties 75 days to complete discovery, but extensions are often granted upon the parties' joint request. In some cases, at the parties' request, OARM has provided the parties with redacted portions of the investigative file received from the Conducting Office, subject to a stipulated protective order. OARM is often called upon by the parties to resolve discovery disputes, including various objections and motions to compel. Discovery is often extensive and may include thousands of pages of documentary evidence for OARM's review. Either party may request a hearing before OARM, which OARM may grant or deny at its discretion. At a hearing on the merits, the parties may call and cross-examine witnesses, and the proceedings are transcribed by a court reporter.

After discovery and any hearing, OARM sets a schedule for briefing on the merits, which typically takes two to four months to complete. To prevail on the merits, a complainant must first prove by a preponderance of the evidence that a protected disclosure was a contributing factor in a personnel action taken or to be taken. This can be proved indirectly:

> OARM may conclude that the disclosure was a contributing factor in the personnel action based upon circumstantial evidence, such as evidence that the employee taking the personnel action knew of the disclosure and that the personnel action occurred within a period of time such that a reasonable person could conclude that the disclosure was a contributing factor in the personnel action.

Id. § 27.4(e)(1). If the complainant meets this burden, OARM will grant corrective relief unless the FBI proves by clear and convincing evidence that it would have taken the same personnel action against the complainant even if he or she had not made the protected disclosure. Id. § 27.4(e)(2).

After any merits hearing and filing of the parties' respective merits (or post-hearing) briefs. OARM renders a final determination on the merits. OARM has broad authority to order corrective relief, which may include

> placing the Complainant, as nearly as possible, in the position he would have been in had the reprisal not taken place; reimbursement for attorneys fees, reasonable costs, medical costs incurred, and travel expenses; back pay and related benefits; and any other reasonable and foreseeable consequential damages.

Id. § 27.4(f). Typically, the parties will submit briefs regarding the appropriateness of specific corrective remedies. A final corrective action order may require OARM to complete complex calculations regarding fees, back pay, and expenses, which in themselves may require additional rounds of briefing.

D. Appeal

Within 30 days of a final determination or corrective action order by OARM, either party may request review by the Deputy Attorney General (DAG), *see* 28 C.F.R. § 27.5, which usually involves another round of briefing. The DAG may set aside or modify OARM's actions, findings, or conclusions found to be arbitrary, capricious, an abuse of discretion, or otherwise not in accordance with law; obtained without procedures required by law, rule, or regulation having been followed; or unsupported by substantial evidence. The DAG has full discretion to review and modify corrective action ordered by OARM. However, if the DAG upholds a finding that there has been a reprisal, then the DAG must order appropriate corrective action.

IV. Statistical Summary

Below is a summary of the disposition of FBI whistleblower reprisal cases filed with OIG, OPR, OARM, and the DAG from the beginning of 2005 through March 15, 2014.

A. OIG

OIG reviewed a total of 89 cases, of which four remained pending as of March 15, 2014. Of the 85 cases that were closed, 010 found that 69 were "non-cognizable." In a significant portion of cases, the claim was found non-cognizable because it was not made to the proper individual or office under 28 C.F.R. § 27.1(a). In other cases, the disclosure did not qualify as protected because it did not allege the type of violation or other misconduct cognizable under the regulations. In another set of cases, the complainant did not allege or suffer a qualifying adverse personnel action as a result of the disclosure. One case was voluntarily dismissed before a decision was made on whether to investigate it.

Of the 69 non-cognizable cases, only three complainants filed a request for corrective action (RCA) with OARM. In two of those cases, OARM found that it lacked jurisdiction to consider the complainants' RCAs. The third case is currently pending before OARM.

OIG determined that the claims of whistleblower reprisal warranted investigation in 15 of the 85 closed matters. Two of these cases were dismissed voluntarily by the complainant after OIG had begun its investigation. In seven cases, OIG determined that there were reasonable grounds to believe that reprisal had been taken against the complainant. In another six cases, 010 did not find reasonable grounds to believe that a reprisal had been or would be taken. Of the four pending cases, 010 has initiated an investigation pursuant to 28 C.F.R. Part 27 in one case and is reviewing the others to determine whether such an investigation is appropriate.

Of the five cases in which OIG found reasonable grounds to believe that reprisal for a protected disclosure had occurred or would occur, three were reported to OARM under 28 C.F.R. § 27.4(a). In two of those cases, OARM found reprisal by the FBI and ordered corrective action. The third case is currently pending before OARM. In the two remaining cases not reported to OARM, one case ended because the FBI agreed to provide corrective relief, and the complainant in the other case did not pursue the matter following 010's finding.

Of the five cases in which OIG found no reasonable grounds to believe that reprisal had been or would be taken, only one complainant proceeded to file an RCA with OARM. That matter is currently pending before OARM.

B. OPR

OPR has received 30 reprisal complaints, of which it has resolved 24. Three complainants pursued RCAs with OARM after waiting the requisite 120 days after filing a complaint with OPR, and three complaints remained pending as of March 15, 2014.

Of the 24 complaints resolved, in only two cases did OPR find that there were reasonable grounds to believe that whistleblower reprisal had been or will be taken. In both cases, OPR forwarded its report to ()ARM. In one of the cases, OARM ultimately concluded that the complainant had failed to prove his allegations. The other case is pending with OARM.

In 16 of the resolved cases, OPR found that it lacked jurisdiction over the claims due to one or more jurisdictional flaws: (1) the complainant complained to a supervisor or other entity, such as the FBI Office of General Counsel, that is not one of the nine individuals or entities listed under 28 C.F.R. § 27.1(a) to receive protected disclosures; (2) the complainant failed to allege a violation of law, mismanagement, gross waste of funds, abuse of authority or a danger to public health or safety; or (3) the alleged protected disclosure occurred after, and thus could not have caused, the alleged reprisal. After OPR terminated its investigation and closed their complaints, three of these 16 complainants filed RCAs with OARM. One is currently pending, OARM dismissed another, and the third was dismissed voluntarily by the complainant.

In another five cases, OPR terminated the investigation after concluding that it lacked reasonable grounds to believe that reprisal occurred. In only one of these five cases did a complainant pursue an RCA with OARM. That matter is currently pending with OARM.

In addition to cases in which OPR either found it lacked jurisdiction or concluded it lacked reasonable grounds to believe reprisal occurred, OPR closed one matter because the complainant did not respond to OPR' s requests for additional information.

In the three cases in which the complainants pursued RCAs with OARM after not hearing within 120 days whether OPR would seek corrective action in their case, two cases were dismissed voluntarily by the complainants. In the third matter, OARM found that the complainant failed to prove the merits of his RCA.

C. OARM

A total of 50 cases have been active before OARM. Of those, 37 have been resolved, and 13 remain pending.

Of the 37 closed matters, OARM dismissed 16 for a lack of jurisdiction. Of these 16 cases, seven complainants failed to exhaust their Conducting Office remedies by failing to file a reprisal complaint with either 010 or OPR prior to filing an RCA with OARM. Three of the dismissed claims were filed by individuals who were neither FBI employees nor applicants for employment. OARM dismissed the remaining six claims for failing to make non-frivolous allegations sufficient for OARM's jurisdiction or for failure to state a claim upon which relief could be granted.

In another 16 cases reviewed by OARM, the complaint established jurisdiction (including one case in which the DAG found on appeal that a complainant had established jurisdiction, reversing OARM' s initial determination that it lacked jurisdiction). Eight of the 16 cases were adjudicated on the merits. In four of these cases, OARM found reprisal by the FBI and ordered corrective relief. In the other four cases, OARM did not find reprisal. Of the remaining eight cases, in four cases the parties reached a settlement after OARM's finding of jurisdiction, and in the other four cases the complainant voluntarily dismissed the case subsequent to OARM's finding of jurisdiction.[2]

In another three cases, the complainants requested voluntary dismissal of their RCAs prior to a jurisdictional determination by OARM. Finally, two additional cases were opened based on complainants' notice of intent to file RCAs, but were closed when no RCAs were ultimately filed.

D. DAG

Seven cases decided by OARM have involved one or more requests for review by the DAG under 28 C.F.R. § 27.5. Three cases involved appeals of OARM's ruling on jurisdiction. In one case, the DAG affirmed OARM's determination that the complainant had failed to establish OARM's jurisdiction over his RCA. In a second case, the DAG reversed OARM's finding that the complainant failed to establish jurisdiction and remanded the matter to OARM. OARM subsequently made a determination that the complainant had proved some, but not all, of his allegations at the merits stage of the proceedings, and ordered corrective relief. The complainant filed an appeal of OARM's decision, which was affirmed by the DAG. In the third case, OARM determined that the complainant had failed to make a nonfrivolous allegation of a protected disclosure sufficient for OARM's jurisdiction. The complainant appealed OARM's decision in that regard, and the matter is currently pending before the DAG.

Three other cases decided by OARM reached the DAG on appeal after OARM's adjudication of the merits of the complainants' RCAs. In one case, the DAG affirmed OARM's determination that the complainant failed to prove the merits of her case. In the second case, both parties appealed portions of °ARM' s final determination (which granted the complainant's RCA) and corrective action order; the DAG ultimately affirmed OARM's decision and ordered corrective relief consistent with that ordered by OARM. In the third case, OARM granted the complainant's RCA and ordered corrective action_ Following the FBI's appeal, the DAG remanded the matter to OARM for further consideration of the legal standard it applied to one of complainant's claims. The DAG eventually affirmed OARM's remand decision, rejecting both sides' appeals, and ordered corrective action.

The seventh case was remanded to OARM for consideration of whether the complainant proved by a preponderance of the evidence that he made a protected disclosure. In that case, OARM had assumed without deciding that the complainant had made a protected disclosure, but ultimately denied the complainant's RCA on the basis that he failed to prove that his alleged protected disclosure was a contributing factor to the personnel action at issue. The matter is currently pending before OARM.

V. The Department's Review and Consultations

This review was led by the Office of the Deputy Attorney General, with participation from the other key participants in administering the Department's FBI whistleblower regulation—the FBI, OARM, OIG, and OPR—as well as the Justice Management Division. In addition, the Department consulted with the Office of Special Counsel and FBI employees, as required by PPD-19, as well as with representatives of non-governmental organizations that support whistleblowers' rights and with private counsel for whistleblowers (collectively, `whistleblower advocates").[3]

For the consultation with FBI employees, the FBI's representatives on the Department's working group consulted with various FBI entities: the Ombudsman; the Office of Equal Employment Opportunity Affairs; the Office of Integrity and Compliance; the Office of Professional Responsibility; the Human Resources Division; and the Inspection Division. The representatives also solicited the views of each of the FBI's three official advisory committees that represent FBI employees—the all-employees advisory committee, the agents committee, and the middle-management committee. In addition, the FBI working group representatives discussed the matter at length with the two co-chairs of the all-employees advisory committee.

The latter co-chairs conveyed two main points, based upon their own prior consultation with various constituents. First, they stated that OARM takes too long to process cases. The co-chairs repeatedly mentioned delays in the OARM process, which they depicted as a serious shortcoming. Second, the co-chairs stated that a better job could be done of making FBI employees conscious of the whistleblower process and its parameters. The co-chairs mentioned specifically that FBI employees may not be aware that, within field offices, a disclosure is protected only if made to the highest-ranking official in the office. The co-chairs recommended that additional trainings or other avenues be explored in order to increase employee knowledge of the rules. The co-chairs also gave the impression that they thought the adjudicators in these cases should be more independent; they implied that use of OARM and the DAG inherently suffered from an appearance-of-bias problem.

VI. Recommended Changes

Below is a discussion of changes to policies and procedures, typically but not necessarily involving changes to the regulations, that the Department believes are warranted.

A. Providing Access to Alternative Dispute Resolution (ADR)

As a result of this review, the Department has created a voluntary mediation program for FBI whistleblower cases. ADR can focus the parties' attention at early stages of litigation, enabling each side to learn more about the other side's goals in a manner that may facilitate early resolution. The Department's Equal Employment Opportunity (EEO) community created the Department of Justice Mediator Corps (DOJMC) Program in 2009 as a means of informal resolution to address and, when possible, resolve workplace disputes. Although the program focuses on EEO issues, the mediators are available to help resolve any type of dispute. Coincidentally, the FBI Office of Equal Opportunity Affairs is responsible for the operational management of the DOJMC program, whose scope is Department-wide. The DOJMC currently has approximately 120 collateral-duty mediators. Roughly two-thirds are FBI employees; the remaining mediators are drawn from across other Department components. Current mediator resources are expected to be sufficient to make available a mediator from outside the FBI should the complainant so desire.

The Department developed and delivered training to a cadre of skilled mediators, and launched the mediation program for FBI whistleblower cases in April 2014. Mediation is available at all stages of the process—i.e., at the Conducting Office level, before OARM, and on any appeal to the Deputy Attorney General. Once mediation is elected, the matter will be stayed. The mediation process should last approximately 90 calendar days, with most mediations taking place within 45 calendar days from the date of election. The mediator will meet with the parties and facilitate discussions in an effort to find common grounds on which to resolve the complaint. If mediation does not result in a settlement, proceedings will resume and the mediator will have no input into the investigation or adjudication of the matter. Nonetheless, the parties are likely to return to the proceedings with a better understanding of what is important to them and to the other party, which may help them reach a settlement later in the process.

OSC actively utilizes mediation in retaliation cases, and offered its strong support for the Department doing so in FBI whistleblower cases.

When revising its regulations, the Department will seek to formalize inclusion of the ADR program, by providing that ADR should be available with the agreement of both the complainant and the FBI from the time of the filing of the initial claim with the Conducting Office and at any subsequent point throughout the process, and that the time periods set forth in the regulations for review and disposition of the claim, as well as for related filings, would be formally stayed pending completion of the mediation process. (Under the current regulations, the Conducting Office's 240-day deadline for completing its investigation and rendering a determination can be extended only if the complainant consents.)

B. Awarding Compensatory Damages

The Department supports amending its regulations to provide that OARM may award compensatory damages, in addition to other available relief. Currently, corrective action ordered by OARM may include:

> placing the Complainant, as nearly as possible, in the position he would have been in had the reprisal not taken place; reimbursement for attorneys fees, reasonable costs, medical expenses incurred, and travel expenses; back pay and related benefits; and any other reasonable and foreseeable consequential damages.

28 C.F.R. § 27.4(f). These categories roughly matched the remedies available to whistleblowers covered by section 2302 at the time when the rule was promulgated. However, the WPEA amended sections 1214 and 1221 to make compensatory damages available for such whistleblowers. *See* Pub. L. 112-199 § 107(b) (amending 5 U.S.C. §§ 1214(g)(2) and 1221(g)(1)(A)(ii)). Likewise, PPD-19 provides that corrective action may include compensatory damages, to the extent authorized by law. PPD-19 at 2.

The Department believes that it is appropriate to amend its regulations to provide for compensatory damages, and has determined that it is authorized to do so by section 2303, which (as amended by the WPA) authorized rulemaking "consistent with applicable provisions" of sections 1214 and 1221. In light of the provision of compensatory damages to whistleblowers covered by section 2302, and PPD-19's direction that covered agencies must make available compensatory damages where authorized by law, the Department intends to amend its regulations accordingly. To be sure, assessment of compensatory damages in a specific case would require examination of additional facts and would necessitate another round of briefing. The

Department will therefore carefully monitor the impact of this expansion of remedies on OARM's case processing pace.

C. Expanding the Definition of Persons to Whom a Protected Disclosure May Be Made

At this time. the Department recommends a limited expansion of the set of persons to whom a "protected disclosure" may be made. Currently, a disclosure is protected if (1) its content qualifies for protection and (2) it was made to one of numerous entities and individuals:

- the Department's Office of Professional Responsibility,
- the Department's Office of the Inspector General, the FBI Office of Professional Responsibility,
- the FBI Inspection Division Internal Investigations Section,
- the Attorney General,
- the Deputy Attorney General,
- the Director of the FBI,
- the Deputy Director of the FBI, or
- the highest-ranking official in any FBI field

office. 28 C.F.R. § 27.1(a).

The Department recommends expanding the persons to whom protected disclosures may be made to include—in addition to the highest-ranking FBI field office official—the second-highest ranking tier of field office officials. Such a change would mean that, in 53 field offices, a disclosure to the Special Agent in Charge (the highest-ranking official) or to any Assistant Special Agent in Charge (the second-highest ranking officials, typically 2-3 per office) would be protected, assuming its content qualified for protection. Further, in the remaining and largest three field offices—Los Angeles, New York City, and Washington, D.C.—a disclosure to the Assistant Director in Charge (the highest-ranking official) or to any Special Agent in Charge (the second-highest ranking official, typically 5-6 in these three offices) would be protected.

This expansion would enhance the ability of employees to make protected disclosures within their own office. At the same time, the limited nature of the expansion would retain the benefit of channeling on-site disclosures to persons with authority to redress wrongdoing once identified. The Department intends to evaluate the impact of this expansion and may choose subsequently to expand further the set of persons to whom a protected disclosure may be made, if it determines that such expansion is warranted.

During the process of reviewing the current FBI whistleblower standards and procedures, the whistleblower advocates recommended revising and broadening the regulations to protect disclosures to any supervisor, noting that PPD-19 instructs IC elements to protect disclosures to any supervisor in the employee's direct chain of command and that the WPEA similarly protects civil-service employees.

OSC, while supportive of the Department's proposed expansion, agrees with the whistleblower advocates that FBI personnel should be protected for making disclosures to other supervisors in the chain of command. OSC recommends that a disclosure should be protected if made to a supervisor at least one level above the employee who may be responsible for the wrongdoing or inefficiency that was disclosed. In OSC's view, whistleblower protection laws are most productive at encouraging the disclosure of wrongdoing, and therefore at making the government more efficient, if protections extend to the employee's specific work site, where most government inefficiencies occur and can be eliminated_ OSC believes that to deny protection unless the disclosure is made to the high-ranked supervisors in the office would undermine a central purpose of whistleblower protection laws.

For now, however, the Department recommends a narrower approach to this issue. The Department believes that the set of persons to whom a protected disclosure can be made is extensive and diverse, and has seen no indication that the list has impeded disclosures of wrongdoing. Indeed, the list of persons and offices to whom a protected disclosure may be made appears on the FBI's Intranet site and is readily findable by any employee who searches that site for "whistleblowing."

D. Improving Training

The Department believes that it is essential that all FBI employees, as well as non-FI31 employees involved in the Department's FBI whistleblower program, receive proper training on the Department's regulations and the rights and responsibilities of all parties. The OIG Whistleblower Ombudsman, in connection with the FBI and other affected offices, is currently reviewing the Department's training efforts regarding whistleblowing activities, and expects to submit recommendations for increasing employee awareness regarding the FBI whistleblower program. The Department will aim to ensure that (1) relevant employees receive appropriate training on a regular basis and (2) employees have ready access at all times to information regarding their rights and responsibilities. Specifically, in light of the discussion in the previous section, the Department will aim to ensure that FBI employees are aware of the various entities and individuals to whom they may make a protected disclosure.

E. Reporting Findings of Wrongdoing

The whistleblower advocates recommended that any final decision that includes a finding of unlawful reprisal be forwarded to OIG, or other appropriate law enforcement authority, for consideration of whether disciplinary action is warranted against the officials responsible for the reprisal. OARM has recently implemented a policy of sending referrals to the FBI Office of Professional Responsibility, with a copy to the FBI Director. The Department believes the regulation should be amended to formalize this practice.

F. Providing Authority to Sanction Violators

The Department supports revising its regulations to allow OARM to sanction litigants who violate protective orders. On several occasions, including in circumstances where the parties have requested the investigative file from the Conducting Office, the parties have agreed to enter a joint stipulated protective order to prevent the release of sensitive law enforcement or privacy-protected information. And although it has yet to have occasion to do so, OARM would issue a protective order if necessary to protect from harassment a witness or other individual who testifies before it.

Because OARM lacks sanction authority, there is currently no recourse available against a party who does not comply with a protective (or other) order, except for possible referral to a bar association. The Department therefore intends to revise its regulations and/or OARM's procedures, as appropriate, to include a provision providing sanction authority similar to that provided to MSPB administrative judges under 5 C.F.R. § 1201.43. Under that provision, MSPB judges may impose sanctions upon the parties "as necessary to serve the ends of justice." As amended in October 2012, *see* 77 FR 62350, 62366, the rule provides that an MSPB judge must provide appropriate prior warning, allow a response to the actual or proposed sanction when feasible, and document in the record the reasons for any resulting sanction. Under the regulation, when a party fails to comply with an order, a judge may:

1) Draw an inference in favor of the requesting party with regard to the information sought;

2) Prohibit the party failing to comply with the order from introducing evidence concerning the information sought, or from otherwise relying upon testimony related to that information;
3) Permit the requesting party to introduce secondary evidence concerning the information sought; and
4) Eliminate from consideration any appropriate part of the pleadings or other submissions of the party that fails to comply with the order.

5 C.F.R. § 1201.43(a).

G. Implementing Acknowledgement and Show Cause Orders

The Department believes that the OARM process could be expedited through use of acknowledgement and show cause orders. The MSPB procedures can serve as a model for this process.

Under OARM's current procedures, 28 C.F.R. § 27.4(c)(1), when a complainant files an RCA with OARM. OARM usually forwards it to the FBI and provides the FBI 25 calendar days to file its response. In some instances, however, the allegations in a complainant's RCA are so deficient that neither OARM nor the FBI can reasonably construe the specific claims raised. In such cases, OARM issues an order requiring the complainant to supplement the RCA to specifically address the elements of a whistleblower claim necessary for OARM's jurisdiction. OARM then forwards the RCA, as supplemented, to the FBI for a response. The complainant is afforded an opportunity to file a reply to the FBI's response, and the FBI is afforded time to file its surreply, if any, thereto. OARM then makes a jurisdictional determination over the complainant's RCA. If OARM finds that it has jurisdiction to consider all or some of complainant's claims, the parties are so notified and are directed to engage in discovery as relevant to the claims over which OARM has jurisdiction.

By contrast, at the MSPB, within three business days of receipt of an appeal, an administrative judge issues an acknowledgment order, which acknowledges receipt of the appeal and informs the parties of the Board's case processing procedures *(e.g.,* pertaining to designating a representative, discovery, filing pleadings, the agency's response, settlement, etc.). In cases where there is an initial question about the Board's jurisdiction, the Board issues, along with the acknowledgment order, an order directing that the appellant show cause as to why the appeal should not be dismissed for lack of jurisdiction. The show cause order puts the parties on full notice of the jurisdictional requirements and their respective burdens of proof In individual right of action cases, the Board orders the appellant to file a statement accompanied by evidence, within 10 calendar days of the date of the order, listing the following:

1) the protected disclosure(s);
2) the date on which the appellant made the disclosure(s);
3) the individual(s) to whom the appellant made the disclosure(s);
4) why the appellant's belief in the truth of the disclosure(s) was reasonable;
5) the action(s) the agency took or failed to take, or threatened to take or fail to take, against the appellant because of the disclosure(s);
6) why the appellant believes that a disclosure was a contributing factor to the action(s); and
7) the date of the appellant's complaint to the Office of Special Counsel (OSC) and the date on which OSC notified the appellant that it was terminating its investigation into the complaint, or if the appellant has not received such notice, evidence that 120 days have passed since the appellant filed a complaint with OSC.

The agency then has 20 calendar days from the date of the order to file its response on the jurisdictional issue. Unless the judge informs the parties otherwise, the record on the issue of jurisdiction will close on the date the agency's response is due. No evidence or argument on jurisdiction filed after that date is accepted unless the submitting party shows that it was not readily available before the record closed.

Implementing similar acknowledgment/show cause orders in FBI whistleblower cases could increase the efficiency of case adjudication at the jurisdictional phase. The acknowledgment order, which would be issued in every case, would notify the parties of OARM's case processing procedures (including its deadlines for filing, the form of and restrictions on pleadings, etc.), the jurisdictional requirements, and the parties' respective burdens of proof at the very beginning of the litigation. Where it appears on the *face* of the RCA that OARM may lack jurisdiction over the matter *(e.g.,* in cases where the complainant failed to exhaust Conducting Office remedies), OARM would give the complainant a very short time period to show cause why the case should not be dismissed, allowing for quick resolution of cases that plainly fail to meet the jurisdictional standard. The FBI would have a specified number of calendar days from the date of the acknowledgement/show cause order to file its response to the complainant's RCA. The FBI's response would be required to include: a statement identifying the FBI's action taken against the complainant and stating the reasons for taking the action; all documents contained in the FBI record of the action; designation and signature by the FBI representative; and any other documents or responses requested by OARM. After receipt of the FBI's response, the record on the jurisdictional issue would close (absent exigent circumstances showing the need for the presentation of additional evidence and/or arguments), thereby eliminating the current practice of providing the parties with the opportunity and time to file reply/surreply briefs. Implementing these procedures would require that the current language pertaining to OARM's initial case processing procedures in 28 C.F.R. § 27.4(c)(1) be revised accordingly.

H. Equalizing Access to Witnesses

The whistleblower advocates who met with the Department raised concerns about access to FBI witnesses. They noted that, in some cases, the FBI has been able to call former FBI management officials or employees as witnesses against the complainant, either through affidavits or testimony at a hearing. However, the complainant has been unable to compel the deposition of those witnesses because OARM lacks authority to compel attendance at a hearing of, or the production of documentary evidence from, persons not currently employed by the Department. *See* 28 C.F.R. § 27.4(e)(3). The Department is considering amending its regulations to prohibit a party from admitting affidavits into evidence from persons who are unavailable for cross-examination at a hearing or deposition, unless an access arrangement has otherwise been made.

G. Expanding Resources

Over the years, concerns have been expressed about the length of time it takes to adjudicate FBI whistleblower cases. With a consistent average of approximately ten new cases a year, the number of active FBI whistleblower cases on OARM's docket at any one time is relatively small. However, the pendency of several large, complex cases among the more routine cases, along with associated administrative responsibilities, significantly slows overall case processing times. Prior to 2005, adjudications were rendered by the Director of OARM with the support of OARM attorneys who were also charged with numerous other duties performed by OARM. This arrangement was found to be impractical and inefficient. In 2005, a full-time attorney position was established to assist the Director in his adjudicatory functions and oversee all whistleblower and related matters.

The functions performed by the staff attorney include, but are not limited to: complaint intake and docketing; record review and organization; legal research; drafting and issuing jurisdictional findings; holding or participating in hearings/teleconferences on discovery issues; ruling on routine motions for extensions of time; setting briefing/hearing schedules; holding or participating in trial-type hearings on the merits of complainants' cases; and drafting final determinations and orders for appropriate corrective relief. The staff attorney also provides significant assistance to attorneys in the Office of the Deputy Attorney General who prepare memoranda to aid the DAG in reviewing cases on appeal. Aside from these adjudicatory functions, the staff attorney is also responsible for the management and oversight of all administrative functions associated with the program, such as records management (including transferring closed case files to the Washington National Records Center/NARA under the appropriate records retention system); maintaining OARM's FBI whistleblower website, docket, case precedent system, and case processing directive; handling Congressional inquiries regarding cases and potential legislation; preparing the annual FBI whistleblower report to the President for the AG's signature; and routinely advising senior level Department officials on OARM's FBI whistleblower procedures and relevant law.

Large, complex cases can slow the adjudicative process due to the multitude of procedural questions that may arise, requests to extend discovery, and extensive factual records that must be reviewed and analyzed after discovery has closed. Such cases complicate the assignment of Department resources in relation to the total case load. A number of cases have taken several years to resolve; the longest case took ten years from the filing of the complaint with 010 to the final decision by the DAG.

During the course of this review, the Department determined that OARM's resources should be expanded. In November 2013, OARM hired a part-time attorney to supplement the work of its full-time staff attorney. In a short period of time, this has enabled faster case processing by OARM.[4]

J. Publishing Decisions

The whistleblower advocates recommended that decisions entered by OARM and the DAG he made available to the public, with appropriate redactions to protect the identities of employees and claimants. They suggested that publication of opinions would help potential whistleblowers provide information in a manner that would be protected and would assist them in litigating their cases should they suffer reprisal. Traditionally, these opinions have not been published due to the presence of law enforcement sensitive and Privacy Act-protected materials. Often, these opinions are highly fact-dependent, with detailed personal information about the claimant inextricably interwoven into the legal analysis. In August 2013, upon a complainant's motion for public disclosure of OARM's Final Determination, OARM for the first time released to the parties for public dissemination a copy of its opinion, which was redacted for Privacy Act protected and law enforcement sensitive information. The Department is exploring whether it is possible, on a broader basis, to publish suitably redacted opinions in a manner that would provide useful information.

K. Publishing Annual Reports

The whistleblower advocates recommended that the Department publish the annual reports that the Attorney General submits to the President pursuant to President Clinton's 1997 memorandum. The Department has no objection to doing so, should the President authorize such publication. The Department has previously disclosed the underlying data contained in the reports (which is essentially what the reports consist of) in response to requests from Congressional staff.

VII. Chums Considered But Rejected

The whistleblower advocates also recommended a number of additional changes that, upon consideration, the Department is not in favor of adopting at this time. These proposals, and the Department's rationale for not adopting them, are discussed below.

A. Allowing Judicial Review

The whistleblower advocates recommended that the regulations be amended to provide a right to judicial review. The Department declines to endorse this suggestion. In passing section 2303, Congress made a deliberate choice to create a closed system for FBI whistleblowers, in contrast to most civil service employees, who received the broader protections of section 2302(h), including access to judicial review. While most employees are protected for disclosures made to the general public, section 2303 provided that disclosures by FBI employees would be protected only if made to the Attorney General or a designee. Had Congress intended for FBI whistleblowers to be subject to judicial review like other agencies, it would have incorporated the FBI into the MSPB process. *See* 64 FR 58783 (quoting 124 Cong. Rec. 28770 (1978) ("We gave [the FBI] special authority . . . to let the President set up their own whistle-blower system so that appeals would not be to the outside but to the Attorney General.") (statement of Representative Udall)). Indeed, every court to have considered the question has concluded that section 2303 does not provide subject matter jurisdiction to hear a challenge to a determination made under the Department's FBI whistleblower regulations. *See McGrath v. Mukasey,* 2008 WL 1781243, *4+ (S.D.N.Y. Apr 18, 2008) (No. 07 CIV. I 1058(SAS)); *Runkle v. Gonzales,* 391 F.Supp.2d 210, 230-34 (D.D.C. 2005); *Roberts v. U.S. Dep't of Justice,* 366 F.Supp.2d 13, 17-23 (D.D.C. 2005). The Department lacks the authority to afford judicial review given the terms of the statute. Moreover, the Department believes that Congress's choice was appropriate given the FBI's involvement in national security work--which has increased dramatically since section 2303 was enacted in 1978—and in law enforcement. The rationale for excluding other agencies from coverage under section 2302 applies to the FBI as well.

B. Using Administrative Law Judges

The whistleblower advocates recommended that adjudications be performed by administrative law judges (ALJs), who are selected pursuant to 5 U.S.C. § 3105, in order to ensure that the adjudications are independent and impartial. The Department agrees, of course, that adjudications must be impartial, but does not believe that Ails are necessary in order to accomplish this. The Department is considering whether it is appropriate to amend its regulations to make explicit what has always been implicit regarding the independence and impartiality of OARM determinations.

C. Imposing Deadlines for Decisions

The whistleblower advocates recommended that OARM's adjudication be subject to a regulatory time limit of 240 days to conduct discovery and convene a hearing, that a decision be issued within 90 days of the close of the record, and that DAG review be limited to 60 days from the completion of briefing. The advocates would allow these time limits to be extended only by consent of the complainant. The Department does not support these revisions at this time. Many cases involve voluminous evidentiary records and present complex factual and legal disputes. As a result, it would be difficult, if not impossible, to meet a strict deadline for adjudication. OARM has recently made procedural changes aimed at decreasing case processing times; if the parties comply with the new stricter discovery deadlines and briefing schedules, OARM believes that it would be possible to adjudicate most cases within one year of receipt (excluding the time needed at the Conducting Office or DAG levels). However, OARM believes that some flexibility is critical, especially when balancing the current resources, case load, and complexity of cases (some of which present thousands of pages of discovery for OARM's review and consideration). Until resource issues can be resolved, it is premature to determine whether and how such a flexible deadline should be constructed. If such a flexible deadline is to be devised, the Department would consider applying it at the DAG level as well.

D. Granting Hearings Upon Request

The whistleblower advocates recommended that OARM grant hearings in all cases upon request. The Department does not believe such a change would be productive. Currently, the decision whether to hold a hearing before OARM is discretionary. In making a determination of whether a protected disclosure was a contributing factor in a personnel action taken or to be taken, the Director of OARM "may hold a hearing at which the Complainant may present evidence in support of his or her claim, in accordance with such procedures as the Director may adopt." 28 C.F.R. § 27.4(e)(1). In practice, OARM has been receptive to requests for a hearing, particularly where the credibility of a witness is at issue. Where a fully developed written record presents a clear basis for a decision, holding a hearing could cause further delay in case resolution.

OSC agrees that hearings may not be necessary in all cases, but suggests adopting a short list of factors for OARM to consider when exercising its discretion on granting or denying a hearing. OSC suggests, for example, that a hearing could be held in cases that depend on witness credibility determinations, cases that require an assessment of employee performance, or where significant whistleblowing disclosures have been made that could reasonably result in retaliation by management.

Of these factors, the Department believes that whether or not witness credibility needed to be assessed is most directly relevant to determining whether a hearing should be held. The Department will consider whether to adopt a list of factors and, if so, whether other factors should be included.

E. Requiring the Production of Any Federal Employee

The whistleblower advocates recommended that OARM procedures be revised to require the production of any current employee of the federal government. (As noted in Part VI.H, OARM may compel attendance at a hearing of, or *the production of documentary evidence from,* only of persons currently employed by the Department.) The Department believes that it lacks *the authority* to make such a change by regulation, and therefore rejects this suggestion.

End Notes

[1] According to press reports at the time, this memorandum was issued during the pendency of a lawsuit filed against the FBI by an employee of the FBI Laboratory who alleged that he had suffered retaliation for disclosing misconduct and sought to avail himself of the expanded remedies offered by the WM. The memorandum was issued one day before the Department's Inspector General issued a report substantiating many of the employee's allegations about misconduct at the FBI Laboratory.

[2] Of the four cases in which the complainant voluntarily dismissed the case subsequent to OARM's finding of jurisdiction, one complainant sought dismissal due to counsel's maternity leave, one sought dismissal to focus on a related Title VII claim in federal court, and one sought dismissal to pursue extended discovery (pursuant to OARM's new case processing directive, see supra at 6, under which OARM will dismiss without prejudice to refiling when additional time is sought to engage in discovery). The record in the fourth case does not reflect the reason for the voluntary dismissal.

[3] The Department convened a meeting with the following whistleblower advocates: Angela Canterbury of the Project on Government Oversight; David Colapinto and Stephen Kahn of Kohn, Kohn & Colapinto; Tom Devine of the Government Accountability Project; Michael German of the American Civil Liberties Union; and Steven Katz, former chief counsel to the chairman of the MSPB.

[4] In addition, OARM has recently revised its policies to address concerns about slow case adjudication, particularly in the area of extended discovery requested by the parties. In a case processing directive issued in October 2011, OARM set specific limits on the type and amount of discovery the parties may conduct, adopting the MSPB's prior procedures and time limits pertaining to the parties' initial disclosures and requests for discovery. Previously, OARM had taken a liberal approach, routinely allowing the parties to engage in extended discovery and present thousands of pages of evidence in support of their respective claims. OARM also would liberally grant motions for extension of discovery deadlines (which had been 90 days from the date on which OARM issued a jurisdictional finding; now, parties are typically afforded 75 days). Now, when the parties request an extended continuation of the time for discovery, OARM has the discretion to dismiss the case without prejudice to filing again after the parties have completed discovery. This procedural option helps to keep cases from languishing on OARM's case docket, while providing the parties the time they need to obtain the discovery they seek. This option is also available in instances where the parties request time to pursue settlement, or where a complainant seeks a stay of OARM proceedings to pursue a Title VII claim in federal court.

In: Whistleblower Protection ...
Editor: Evelyn Brooks

ISBN: 978-1-63483-147-5

Chapter 9

INTELLIGENCE WHISTLEBLOWER PROTECTIONS: IN BRIEF*

Rodney M. Perry

SUMMARY

Intelligence whistleblowers are generally Intelligence Community (IC) employees or contractors who bring to light allegations of agency wrongdoings by, for example, disclosing information on such wrongdoings to congressional intelligence committees. Such disclosures can aid oversight of, or help curb misconduct within, intelligence agencies. However, intelligence whistleblowers could face retaliation from their employers for their disclosures, and the fear of such retaliation may deter whistleblowing. Congress and President Obama have taken measures to protect certain intelligence whistleblowers from retaliation, and thereby seemingly encourage these whistleblowers to disclose information on agency wrongdoing. These measures are the Intelligence Community Whistleblower Protection Act of 1998 (ICWPA), Presidential Policy Directive 19 (PPD-19), and Title VI of the Intelligence Authorization Act of 2014 (Title VI). Each of these measures details what disclosures fall within the scope of its protections, which generally include certain disclosures through government channels (e.g., disclosures to agency inspectors general or congressional intelligence

* This is an edited, reformatted and augmented version of a Congressional Research Service publication R43765, prepared for Members and Committees of Congress, dated October 23, 2014.

committees). None of these measures protect against retaliation or potential criminal liability arising from disclosures to media sources. The ICWPA applies to both IC employees and contractors, whereas PPD-19 and Title VI appear to apply only to IC employees.

The ICWPA is the oldest of the three intelligence whistleblower protections and, of the three, provides the least amount of protection to those falling within its scope. The ICWPA does not explicitly prohibit retaliation against IC whistleblowers. Rather, it outlines procedures through which whistleblowers can disclose to the congressional intelligence committees information on "urgent concerns," such as violations of law or false statements to Congress. The ICWPA further contains no explicit mechanism for obtaining a remedy for retaliation stemming from disclosure of an urgent concern to Congress. It merely allows an IC whistleblower who has faced an adverse personnel action because he disclosed an urgent concern to the congressional intelligence committees to then use the ICWPA's disclosure procedures to inform the committees of the retaliation.

PPD-19, unlike the ICWPA, expressly prohibits an IC employee from taking an adverse personnel action or security clearance determination against another employee because of a protected disclosure. It additionally requires intelligence agencies to develop procedures for internally investigating, through agency Inspectors General, allegations of impermissible retaliation. After finding that impermissible retaliation has occurred, Inspectors General can recommend that agency heads take corrective action. When an employee has exhausted the internal review procedures that must be established under PPD-19, he can appeal to the Director of National Intelligence, who then has the discretion to convene a review panel. If it finds that improper retaliation occurred, the review panel can recommend that the agency head take remedial action.

Title VI seemingly codifies, and expands upon, some of the protections of PPD-19. Its protections, and modes of enforcement, differ depending on the type of retaliation alleged. More specifically, Title VI's protected disclosures and enforcement methods in the context of allegations of adverse personnel action are distinct from its protected disclosures and enforcement methods for allegations of adverse security clearance or information access determinations.

INTRODUCTION

Generally speaking, whistleblowers are those who expose misconduct (e.g., fraud, abuse, or illegal activity) within an organization. In the context of the Intelligence Community (IC), whistleblowers are generally employees or contractors of federal intelligence agencies who bring to light information on agency wrongdoings. Whistleblowers disclose this information through government channels (e.g., the congressional intelligence committees or agency inspectors general) or to the media. Such disclosures can aid oversight of, and thereby curb misconduct within, intelligence agencies. When an IC whistleblower discloses information on alleged agency wrongdoing, he could face retaliation from his employer by, for example, being fired, demoted, or having his security clearance revoked.

The threat of retaliation may deter potential whistleblowers from disclosing information on agency wrongdoing. There is seemingly tension between the desire to eliminate this deterrence, and thus encourage whistleblowers to bring agency misconduct to light, and the need to protect government secrets which, if disclosed publicly, could be harmful to the country's national security interests. Apparently seeking to strike balance within this tension, Congress and President Obama have taken action to limit retaliation against IC whistleblowers for certain types of protected disclosures, which do not include disclosures to media sources. That is, IC whistleblowers who disclose information to media sources generally are unprotected against potential retaliation or criminal sanction.

There are three sources of protections against retaliation for IC whistleblowers: the Intelligence Community Whistleblower Protection Act of 1998 (ICWPA),[1] Presidential Policy Directive 19 (PPD-19),[2] and Title VI of the Intelligence Authorization Act for Fiscal Year 2014 (Title VI).[3] Before passing the ICWPA, which is the oldest of the three protections, Congress observed that intelligence whistleblowers apparently lacked protection against retaliation stemming from their disclosures of agency wrongdoings.[4] Whistleblower protections for federal employees are largely governed by the Whistleblower Protection Act (WPA), which Congress initially passed in 1989, and its amendments.[5] The WPA expressly excluded intelligence agency employees from its applicability, and thus initially left intelligence whistleblowers unprotected against retaliation.[6] The ICWPA seemingly represented Congress's attempt at filling this gap by extending protections to intelligence whistleblowers.

Though the ICWPA extended some protections to intelligence whistleblowers, it afforded such whistleblowers less protection than the WPA affords non-intelligence whistleblowers. However, protections for intelligence whistleblowers have strengthened over time. PPD-19, which President Obama issued in 2012, expanded upon the ICWPA's protections for some IC whistleblowers, and Title VI generally codified, and in some instances built upon, the protections of PPD-19. This report describes these three sources of IC whistleblower protection.

Intelligence Community Whistleblower Protection Act of 1998

The ICWPA is the oldest of the three intelligence whistleblower protections. In passing the ICWPA, Congress observed that the threat of adverse personnel action to IC employees deterred them from whistleblowing.[7] This deterrence from whistleblowing, Congress found, may have been constricting the flow of information to congressional intelligence committees that the committees needed to properly perform their oversight responsibilities.[8] The ICWPA therefore permits IC employees and contractors to bring a complaint or disclose specified information to Congress, and outlines the procedures for doing so. However, the ICWPA does not expressly prohibit retaliation against IC whistleblowers for permissibly bringing a complaint or information to Congress and contains no explicit mechanism for obtaining a remedy for this retaliation. Rather, the ICWPA merely allows an IC whistleblower who has faced such retaliation to then use the act's disclosure procedures to inform the intelligence committees that the retaliation has occurred.

The ICWPA applies to employees of the Central Intelligence Agency, Defense Intelligence Agency, National Imagery and Mapping Agency, National Reconnaissance Office, National Security Agency, Federal Bureau of Investigation, and any other agency that the President determines has the principal function of conducting foreign intelligence or counterintelligence activities.[9] The ICWPA also applies to the employees of a contractor of any of the aforementioned agencies.[10] An employee seeking to bring a complaint or disclose information to Congress under the ICWPA is subject to two limitations: (1) the complaint or information must be related to an "urgent concern" as defined in the act; and (2) the employee must first bring the complaint or disclose the information to the agency head through the proper agency channels.

Under the ICWPA, IC employees and contractors can disclose to Congress only complaints and information that are "with respect to an urgent concern."[11] Under the act, an "urgent concern" can be one of three things.[12] First, it can be a "serious or flagrant" abuse, problem, violation of executive order or law, or deficiency in funding, agency administration, or agency operations involving classified information.[13] Second, an urgent concern can be a false statement to, or willful withholding from, Congress on an issue of material fact relating to intelligence activity funding, administration, or operation.[14] Third, an urgent concern can include adverse personnel action stemming from disclosure under the ICWPA.[15] A complaint or information that is not regarding one of these three "urgent concerns" is not covered by the ICWPA.[16]

IC employees and contractors must first bring complaints or information regarding "urgent concerns" to the agency head through proper agency channels, as described in the ICWPA, before bringing them to Congress. This generally requires first bringing a complaint or information to the agency's Inspector General or the Inspector General of the IC (IGIC),[17] who then has 14 calendar days to evaluate the credibility of the complaint or information.[18] Upon finding the complaint or information credible, the Inspector General must send notice of its finding, along with the complaint or information, to the agency head within the 14-calendar-day period for evaluation.[19] The agency head then has 7 calendar days from receipt of the Inspector General's notice to forward the notice, along with any of the agency head's comments, to the congressional intelligence committees.[20]

The ICWPA allows employees to contact intelligence committees directly if the Inspector General either does not find the complaint or information credible, or sends the agency head an inaccurate complaint or inaccurate information.[21] However, this ability to contact the intelligence committees directly is subject to two limitations. First, before making such contact, an employee or contractor must give the agency head a statement of the complaint or information through the Inspector General, along with notice of intent to contact the intelligence committees directly.[22] Second, the employee or contractor must follow the agency head's direction, given through the Inspector General, on compliance with appropriate security practices when contacting the intelligence committees.[23]

The ICWPA seemingly represents an attempt by Congress to fill a gap in federal whistleblower protections by extending such protections to IC whistleblowers where they were expressly excluded from the WPA and its amendments, which generally provide whistleblower protections to federal employees.[24] However, the ICWPA appears to afford IC whistleblowers fewer protections than the WPA affords non-intelligence whistleblowers. The WPA provides an employee with an individual right of action for prohibited retaliation, through which he can bring a claim against this agency in the Merit

Systems Protection Board (MSPB).[25] The MSPB can then provide several remedies, including, but not limited to, returning the individual to the position he would have been in if retaliation had not occurred, awarding back pay, and awarding any reasonable and foreseeable consequential damages.[26] If an employee's claim is unsuccessful before the MSPB, the employee can appeal the MSPB's decision to the U.S. Court of Appeals for the Federal Circuit.[27]

Conversely, the ICWPA provides no explicit mechanism for remedying for retaliation stemming from disclosure of an urgent concern to Congress; it merely prescribes the process through which such disclosures can be made and allows employees and contractors to then use those disclosure procedures to inform Congress of any resulting improper retaliation. Further, the ICWPA expressly states that Inspector General and agency head action taken pursuant to the ICWPA is not subject to judicial review, unlike retaliation claims under the WPA.[28] In comparing the ICWPA's protections against the WPA's, some commentators have questioned the ICWPA's effectiveness at protecting intelligence whistleblowers from improper retaliation.[29]

PRESIDENTIAL POLICY DIRECTIVE 19

President Obama issued PPD-19 on October 10, 2012, to ensure that IC employees can effectively report instances of waste, fraud, and abuse.[30] PPD-19 protects *employees* who engage in "protected disclosures" from certain types of adverse action by their employers. Thus, unlike the ICWPA, PPD-19's protections do not appear to extend to IC contractors. Under PPD-19, five types of disclosures fall under the umbrella of "protected disclosures." First, protected disclosures include employee disclosures to the agency Inspector General, Director of National Intelligence, IGIC, or supervisors within the employee's direct chain-of-command.[31] The employee must reasonably believe that disclosures to such persons evidence (1) a perceived violation of law, rule, or regulation; (2) gross mismanagement; (3) gross waste of funds; (4) abuse of authority; or (5) a specific and substantial threat to public health or safety.[32] Second, PPD-19 protects disclosures to congressional committees made pursuant to the ICWPA, discussed above.[33] Third, "protected disclosures" comprise any disclosure of a violation of PPD-19.[34] Fourth, protected disclosures include those made pursuant to an investigation or proceeding involving a violation of PPD-19.[35] Finally, the definition of "protected disclosures" generally includes disclosures to Inspectors General.[36]

Under PPD-19, intelligence agency[37] employees who make protected disclosures cannot consequently be subject to adverse personnel actions[38] or have their access to classified information negatively affected by an officer or employee of the agency.[39] PPD-19 required intelligence agencies to certify, within 270 days of its issuance, that they had internal procedures for reviewing allegations of wrongful personnel actions or impacts on access to classified information.[40] These procedures must provide for the protection of classified information and intelligence sources and methods.[41] PPD-19 requires that agency procedures permit agency Inspectors General to review employee allegations of adverse personnel action or improper restriction of access to classified information and recommend agency heads take corrective action if a violation of PPD-19 has occurred.[42] Such corrective action can include (but is not limited to) reinstatement, back pay, and attorney's fees.[43] Once an agency head receives an Inspector General's recommendation, PPD-19 requires he "carefully consider" the recommendation and findings and decide whether or not corrective action is appropriate.[44]

After employees exhaust the internal agency review process, PPD-19 allows them to request external review to the IGIC acting on behalf of the Director of National Intelligence.[45] Once such a request is made, the IGIC can, within his or her discretion, convene an external review panel.[46] Such a panel consists of the ICIG plus two Inspectors General that the ICIG chooses from the Departments of State, the Treasury, Defense, Justice, Energy, Homeland Security, or the CIA, exclusive of the Inspector General of the agency that internally reviewed the retaliation claim.[47] The panel then has 180 days to determine whether improper retaliation occurred.[48] If the panel concludes that such retaliation did happen, it can recommend that the agency head take corrective action, and the agency head must "carefully consider" this recommendation.[49] The agency head then has 90 days to inform the panel and the Director of National Intelligence of what, if any, action it takes.[50] The Director of National Intelligence must notify the President if the agency head does not tell the Director what action he takes within the allotted 90-day window.[51] PPD-19 further requires the IGIC to report annually all panel determinations and recommendations, along with agency head responses, to the Director of National Intelligence and, "as appropriate, to the relevant congressional committees."[52]

PPD-19 offers intelligence whistleblowers falling within its scope more protection against retaliation than the ICWPA. By allowing IC employees and contractors to disclose retaliation via adverse personnel action to congressional intelligence committees, the ICWPA purports to protect against only adverse personnel action; unlike PPD-19, it makes no mention of adverse security clearance determinations. Further, PPD-19, unlike the ICWPA, expressly prohibits retaliation against IC whistleblowers who make protected disclosures, whereas the ICWPA merely outlines the process through which such disclosures can be made.

Although PPD-19 offers intelligence whistleblowers more protection against retaliation than the ICWPA, it is unclear how effective PPD-19 will be in curbing such retaliation. Under PPD-19, the initial review of an improper retaliation allegation occurs within the agency wherein the whistleblower allegedly faced retaliation. This could raise questions regarding the initial review's impartiality, and thus effectiveness at achieving accurate results. Further, though PPD-19 appears to attempt to counteract impartiality in reviewing retaliation claims by creating an external review panel to whom such claims can eventually go, this external review panel cannot mandate that agency heads take corrective action after finding that impermissible retaliation occurred. Rather, this external review panel can only recommend that agency heads take corrective action. The agency head is then free to disregard the board's recommendation. Finally, as with all presidential policy directives or executive orders, President Obama (or any future Presidents) can revoke or modify it at any time.[53]

TITLE VI OF THE INTELLIGENCE AUTHORIZATION ACT FOR FY2015

On July 7, 2014, Congress enacted the Intelligence Authorization Act for FY2014,[54] which included protections for IC whistleblowers at Title VI of the act. Title VI seemingly codifies some of PPD-19's protections and, under specified circumstances, expands upon them. Like PPD-19, Title VI's protections extend only to *employees* of "covered intelligence community element[s],"[55] and therefore do not appear to apply to IC contractors.[56] Title VI's protections are bifurcated: it protects whistleblowers from retaliation in the form of both adverse personnel actions and adverse security clearance or information access determinations resulting from their making protected disclosures. Whether or not a disclosure is protected under Title VI depends on what is being disclosed to whom, and protected disclosures and enforcement mechanisms under the act differ in the context of retaliation via adverse personnel actions and adverse security clearance or information access determinations.

Protection from Adverse Personnel Actions

Under Title VI, disclosures for which an employee is protected against retaliation in the form of adverse personnel action include those made to (1) the Director of National Intelligence (or his or her designee); (2) the IGIC (or his or her designee); (3) the head of the employing agency (or his or her designee); (4) the employing agency's Inspector General; (5) congressional intelligence committees; or (6) a member of a congressional intelligence committee.[57] For Title VI to protect an employee against adverse personnel action, the disclosure must be of information that the employee reasonably believes evidences a violation of federal laws or regulations, mismanagement, waste of funds, abuse of authority, or a substantial and specific danger to public health or safety.[58] Title VI does not contain any mechanism to enforce its protection against retaliation by adverse personnel action; it merely prohibits agency employees from taking adverse personnel action against other employees who make protected disclosures.[59] Enforcement is expressly left to the President.[60] It is unclear whether the President will develop new enforcement procedures, or will utilize enforcement procedures that already exist (i.e., PPD-19's enforcement procedures).

Protection from Adverse Security Clearance and Information Access Determinations

Under Title VI, an IC employee cannot take adverse security clearance action against another employee, or restrict the other employee's access to classified information, because the employee made a protected disclosure.[61] The disclosures for which an employee cannot face adverse security clearance actions or access determinations differ from the disclosures for which an employee cannot face adverse personnel actions.[62] In the context of adverse security clearance actions or access determinations, Title VI's umbrella of protected disclosures includes a number of lawful communications. First, it includes communications to the Director of National Intelligence, agency head, or agency Inspector General (or their respective designees) that the employee reasonably believes evidences a violation of federal laws or regulations, gross mismanagement, waste of funds, abuse of authority, or a substantial and specific danger to public health or safety.[63] Second, it includes disclosures made in accordance with the procedures outlined in the ICWPA, discussed above.[64] Finally, Title VI protects disclosures made while exercising a legal right of appeal or complaint (including testimony in connection with someone else exercising such a right) or cooperating with an Inspector General.[65] However, disclosures within this third category fall within Title VI only if they do not result in the sharing of information that is classified under an executive order for national security reasons.[66]

Title VI's protections against adverse security or information access determinations also differ from its protections against adverse personnel actions because it provides mechanisms for enforcing the former; whereas enforcement of the latter is left to the President's discretion as mentioned above. Title VI directed the President to select, within 180 days of the statute's enactment (July 7, 2014), an agency or department responsible for ensuring that intelligence agencies have adequate procedural protections that they must follow before taking action that adversely affects an employee's security clearance or information access.[67] Within this time frame, the President must also select an agency or department responsible for developing procedures that agencies must follow for employee appeals of adverse security clearance or information access decisions to the ICIG or agency Inspector General.[68] Title VI permits an employee 90 days from the adverse security clearance or information determination to use these appeal procedures.[69]

The appeal procedures that must be established under Title VI must allow the ICIG or agency Inspector General to engage in a fact-finding investigation and report the investigation results to the agency head within 180 days of the employee's appeal.[70] During the investigation, the employee must be allowed, "to the fullest extent possible," to present relevant evidence.[71] The ICIG or agency Inspector General cannot find that a prohibited security clearance or information access determination occurred if the agency demonstrates that the employee's disclosure was not a contributing factor in the determination.[72] The agency can demonstrate such by establishing, by a preponderance of the evidence, that it would have taken the same action absent the employee's protected disclosures.[73] Under the preponderance of the evidence standard, it appears as though the agency must show that it is more likely than unlikely that the agency would have taken the same action against the employee absent the employee's disclosures.[74] In evaluating the agency's contributing factor evidence, Title VI requires the ICIG or agency Inspector General to afford the "utmost deference" to the agency's judgments regarding threats to national security.[75] If the ICIG or agency Inspector General determines that a prohibited security clearance or information access determination occurred and reports its determination to the agency head, the agency head "shall" take corrective action.[76]

If, however, the ICIG or agency Inspector General finds that no improper adverse security clearance or information access determination occurred, Title VI requires that the employee be given 60 days to externally appeal such a finding.[77] Title VI does not contain substantive requirements for this external appeal.[78] Rather, through the statute, Congress mandated that the Director of National Intelligence, in consultation with the Attorney General and the Secretary of Defense, develop and implement procedures for adjudicating external appeals.[79] As of this writing, the Director of National Intelligence does not appear to have developed these appeal procedures. Though Title VI does not contain substantive requirements for appeal procedures, it does require the Director of National Intelligence to inform the congressional intelligence committees when he issues an appeal order under the procedures that he develops.[80]

Title VI seemingly expands PPD-19's protections against retaliation in the form of adverse security clearance or information access determinations by introducing additional enforcement mechanisms. For example, Title VI requires adequate protections prior to adverse security clearance or information access determinations, where PPD-19 does not. However, Title VI does not appear to strengthen PPD-19's protections against retaliation in the form of adverse personnel action, as it leaves enforcement of such protections to the President.

End Notes

[1] P.L. 105-272, 112 Stat. 2396 (1998).

[2] OFFICE OF THE WHITE HOUSE PRESS SECRETARY, PRESIDENTIAL POLICY DIRECTIVE 19- PROTECTING WHISTLEBLOWERS WITH ACCESS TO CLASSIFIED INFORMATION (Oct. 10, 2012), hereinafter PPD-19.

[3] P.L. 113-126, 128 Stat. 1390, 1414 (2014).

[4] See S.Rept. 105-165, at 2 (1998).

[5] P.L. 101-12, 103 Stat. 16 (1989).

[6] The WPA, by its text, does not apply to employees of "the Federal Bureau of Investigation, the Central Intelligence Agency, the Defense Intelligence Agency, the National Geospatial-Intelligence Agency, the National Security Agency, the Office of the Director of National Intelligence, and the National Reconnaissance Office." 5 U.S.C. §2302(a)(2)(C).

[7] See P.L. 105-272, §701-02, 112 Stat. 2396, 2413 (1998).

[8] Id.

[9] The ICPWA provisions relating to employees and contractors of the Central Intelligence Agency (CIA) are at 50 U.S.C. §3517(d)(5). The parallel ICPWA provisions relating to employees and contractors of the Defense Intelligence Agency, National Imagery and Mapping Agency, National Reconnaissance Office, National Security Agency, Federal Bureau of Investigation, and any other agency that the President determines has the principal function of conducting foreign intelligence or counterintelligence activities are at 5 U.S.C. app. §8H.

[10] 50 U.S.C. §3517(d)(5)(A); 5 U.S.C. app. §8H(a)(1)(A), (B).

[11] 50 U.S.C. §3517(d)(5)(A); 5 U.S.C. app. §8H(a)(1)(A), (B).

[12] 50 U.S.C. §3517(d)(5)(g); 5 U.S.C. app. §8H(h)(1).

[13] 50 U.S.C. §3517(d)(5)(g)(i)(I); 5 U.S.C. app. §8H(h)(1)(A). It cannot, however, be a difference in opinion on public policy matters. 50 U.S.C. §3517(d)(5)(g)(i)(I); 5 U.S.C. app. §8H(h)(1)(A)

[14] 50 U.S.C. §3517(d)(5)(g)(i)(II); 5 U.S.C. app. §8H(h)(1)(B).

[15] 50 U.S.C. §3517(d)(5)(g)(i)(III); 5 U.S.C. app. §8H(h)(1)(C).

[16] See 50 U.S.C. §3517(d)(5)(A); see also 5 U.S.C. app. §8H(a)(1)(A), (B).

[17] 50 U.S.C. §3517(d)(5)(A); 5 U.S.C. app. §8H(a)(1)(A), (B). Inspectors General are generally intended to provide independent, objective audits and investigations of agency operations, among other things. See 50 U.S.C. §3517(a); see also 5 U.S.C. app. §2. The Inspector General of the IC is responsible for, among other things, conducting independent investigations, inspections, and audits of programs and activities that the Director of National Intelligence is responsible for administering. 50 U.S.C. §3033(b).

[18] 50 U.S.C. §3517(d)(5)(B); 5 U.S.C. app. §8H(b).

[19] 50 U.S.C. §3517(d)(5)(B); 5 U.S.C. app. §8H(b).

[20] 50 U.S.C. §3517(d)(5)(C); 5 U.S.C. app. §8H(c). "Congressional intelligence committees" refers to the Senate Select Committee on Intelligence and the House Permanent Select Committee on Intelligence. 50 U.S.C. §3517(a)(4); 5 U.S.C. app. §8H(h)(2).

[21] 50 U.S.C. §3517(d)(5)(D)(i); 5 U.S.C. app. §8H(d)(1). When an employee contacts a committee member or employee directly, the committee member or employee "receives [the] complaint or information ... in that member or employee's official capacity as a member or employee of that committee." 50 U.S.C. §3517(d)(5)(D)(iii); 5 U.S.C. app. §8H(d)(3).

[22] 50 U.S.C. §3517(d)(5)(D)(ii)(I); 5 U.S.C. app. §8H(d)(2)(A).

[23] 50 U.S.C. §3517(d)(5)(D)(ii)(II); 5 U.S.C. app. §8H(d)(2)(B).

[24] The WPA, by its text, does not apply to employees of "the Federal Bureau of Investigation, the Central Intelligence Agency, the Defense Intelligence Agency, the National Geospatial-Intelligence Agency, the National Security Agency, the Office of the Director of National Intelligence, and the National Reconnaissance Office." 5 U.S.C. §2302(a)(2)(C).

[25] 5 U.S.C. §1221.

[26] Id. at (g)(1)(A). The MSPB is an independent, quasi-judicial government agency that, among other things, "adjudicat[es] Federal employee appeals of agency personnel actions ..." 5 C.F.R. §1200.1.

[27] See 5 U.S.C. §1214(c).

[28] 50 U.S.C. §3517(d)(5)(F); 5 U.S.C. app. §8H(f).

[29] See, e.g., Mary-Rose Papandrea, Leaker Traitor Whistleblower Spy: National Security Leaks and the First Amendment, 94 B.U. L. Rev. 449, 493 (2014) (observing that "... the ICWPA arguably fails to provide any real protection ..."); See Richard Moberly, Whistleblowers and the Obama Presidency: the National Security Dilemma, 16 Emp. Rts. & Emp. Pol'y J. 51, 109 (2012) (detailing perceived gaps in the protections that the ICWPA affords intelligence whistleblowers).

[30] PPD-19 at 1. Presidential policy directives are binding on executive agencies and, in practice, can be equivalent to executive orders. See Ctr. for Effective Gov't v. Department of State, No. 13-0414, 2013 WL 6641262, at *2, n. 3 (D.D.C. Dec. 17, 2013) ("even though issued as a directive, the PPD-6 carries the force of law as policy guidance to be implemented by recipient agencies, and it is the functional equivalent of an Executive Order.").

[31] PPD-19 at 7.

[32] Id.

[33] See id.

[34] Id.

[35] Id. at 8.

[36] Id.

[37] More specifically, PPD-19 applies to so-called "Covered Agenc[ies]", which it defines as an executive department or independent establishment that contains an "Intelligence Community Element," including the Central Intelligence Agency, National Security Agency, Defense Intelligence Agency, National Geospatial-Intelligence Agency, National Reconnaissance Office, and any other agency that the President determines has as its principal function the conduct of foreign intelligence or counterintelligence activities. Id. at 6. The directive explicitly states that the Federal Bureau of Investigations is not a "Covered Agency." Id.

[38] Prohibited personnel actions include, but are not limited to, transfer, reassignment, demotion, suspension, termination, and negative decisions regarding pay or benefits. Id.

[39] Id. at 2-3.

[40] Id. PPD-19 mandates that such review processes apply to any actions arising after the date on which the intelligence agency head certifies the agency review process. Id.

[41] Id.

[42] Id.

[43] Id.

[44] Id.

[45] Id. at 4. The Director of National Intelligence is a presidential appointee "subject to the authority, direction, and control of the President" who, among other things, advises the President, National Security Council, and Homeland Security Council on intelligence matters related to national security. 50 U.S.C. §3023.

[46] PPD-19 at 4.

[47] Id.

[48] Id.

[49] Id.

[50] Id.

[51] Id.

[52] Id.

[53] See CRS Report RS20846, Executive Orders: Issuance, Modification, and Revocation, by Vivian S. Chu and Todd Garvey.

[54] P.L. 113-126, 128 Stat. 1390 (2014).

[55] Covered agencies include the Central Intelligence Agency, National Geospatial-Intelligence Agency, Office of the Director of National Intelligence, Defense Intelligence Agency, National Security Agency, and the National Reconnaissance Office. 50 U.S.C. §3234(a)(2).

[56] See 50 U.S.C. §3234(b); 50 U.S.C. §3341(j)(1).

[57] 50 U.S.C. §3234(b).

[58] Id.

[59] 50 U.S.C. §3234(b).

[60] 50 U.S.C. §3234(c).

[61] 50 U.S.C. §3341(j)(1).

[62] Compare 50 U.S.C. §3234(b) with 50 U.S.C. §3341(j)(1)(A)-(D).

[63] 50 U.S.C. §3341(j)(1)(A),(B).

[64] 50 U.S.C. §3341(j)(1)(C).

[65] 50 U.S.C. §3341(j)(1)(D).

[66] Id.

[67] 50 U.S.C. §3341(b)(7)(B).

[68] 50 U.S.C. §3341(b)(7)(A); P.L. 113-126, §602(a)(2), 128 Stat. 1390, 1416-17 (2014).

[69] 50 U.S.C. §3341(j)(4)(A).

[70] P.L. 113-126, §602(a)(2), 128 Stat. 1390, 1416-17 (2014).

[71] Id.

[72] 50 U.S.C. §3341(j)(4)(C).

[73] Id.

[74] See Concrete Pipe and Prods. of Cal v. Constr. Laborers Pension Trust of S. Cal., 508 U.S. 602, 622 (observing that showing a fact by a preponderance of the evidence "simply requires the trier of fact to believe that the existence of a fact is more probable than its nonexistence ...") (internal quotations omitted).

[75] Id.

[76] 50 U.S.C. §3341(j)(4)(B). This corrective action must, as "nearly as practicable and reasonable," put the employee in the position he would have been in but-for the prohibited retaliation and can include compensatory damages of up to $300,000. Id.

[77] 50 U.S.C. §3341(j)(5)(A).

[78] See id.

[79] 50 U.S.C. §3341(j)(5)(B).

[80] 50 U.S.C. §3341(j)(5)(C).

INDEX

D

E

L

M

N

O

P

R

S

T

U

V

W